Women on Pilgrimage

Women on Pilgrimage

Edited by Shurden, Nutt, Dinwiddie, McEwen

BROADMAN PRESS
Nashville, Tennessee

© Copyright 1982 • Broadman Press.

4254-28

ISBN: 0-8054-5428-4

Dewey Decimal Classification: 248.843

Subject Headings: WOMEN//CHRISTIAN LIFE

Library of Congress Catalog Card Number: 81-70975

Printed in the United States of America

To Vera Peterson

Whose bright faith
Has lighted the pathway—

Whose gentle example
Has called us to follow—

Whose selfless concern
Has given the Christ a face.

Contents

Women on Pilgrimage Through Choice

Introduction

Life was supposed to be easy. If we just lived right, were kind and loving, went to church, and did what was expected of us, we would find the happiness that our mothers and grandmothers modeled for us. Somehow, it didn't turn out that way. Childhood fantasies turned into painful realities in adulthood. Relationships were fractured. Children chose life-styles we didn't want for them. Loved ones suffered. Roles and expectations changed. That happy, close-knit family that lived happily ever after was an elusive dream for many.

Most of us discovered that pain and loss were as much a part of life as joy and celebration. The clichés from childhood weren't enough to get us through the difficult days. Instead, we began to look for guidance from Christian women who had struggled with life's crises, who had grown in the process and found strength and courage for the journey. In this book women speak candidly about their own crucial life events and how they dealt with them in the context of their Christian faith.

Each woman brings to her experience her own abilities to cope, to grow, to change, to deal with failure, to make choices. Each has in common an underlying faith in Christ as Savior and Sustainer; this faith has been crucial in her life experiences.

The reader will not find easy answers to the experiences described in this book. Rather, the doubts, fears, and hard realities that are a part of the struggles in our daily lives will be apparent. We are unique, but our experiences are not. We are Christians, but some of us have questioned our most basic beliefs. At times, we have felt totally alone in our pain. Then we experienced the healing that comes with a new awareness of God at work in our lives and the acceptance and affirmation that can come from Christian friends.

We believe that the process of growth usually involves pain. We also believe that pain can be somewhat alleviated by reading about other Christians' similar crises and how they coped and came through.

The life experiences of the women in this book fall into three categories. The first one involves different *crises* that women faced: suicidal depression, divorce, or death of a spouse. The events were so painful that the women had to either grow beyond the crises or be physically or emotionally destroyed by them. They tell of their growth beyond pain.

The second category involves *changes* that women made in their lives. This category, too, involves the pain of risk and uncertainty. In moving toward personal fulfillment and developing her gifts, each woman describes the changes she made: to return to school, to resume a career, to change careers, or to seek professional therapy. The changes brought pain and risk, but ultimately growth.

The final category involves *choices* made by women. These are choices that affected stages and periods of their lives. Some are lifetime choices. Chapters on singleness, dual careers, identity, personhood, interrupting a career, and mid-life are found in this section.

The editors and contributors to this book believe that the Christian life is a pilgrimage. We all have different routes, setbacks, resources, detours, and purposes. One thing we have in common: our Companion on the journey. Also, we have each other for comfort and encouragement along the way.

Our prayer is that our stories may give strength for your journey.

Women on Pilgrimage
Through Crisis

1

Depression

Dorothy Hays Steedly

The cold winter rain drummed against the window. I sat on the side of the bed and wept as I tried to deal once more with the depression that seemed never to go away. Its gnawing, drilling intolerable pain was at its peak, and I was desperately afraid I could not handle the torture much longer. The gun lay in the drawer! Ten minutes before it had been in my hands directed at myself. My mind ached from its endless struggle with the black cloud which hovered over my existence. I felt as though I were all alone, isolated from friends and family, detached from surroundings. In a deep, endless tunnel I carried on a constant upward struggle and reached for an occasional glimmer of light at the far end. It had gone on so long that I no longer wanted to fight. I wanted rest and some kind of peace.

"God (if there is one), show me a way!" As I cried and prayed my mind traveled back over several months, and I remembered a session with my therapist. I was talking of my need for the support of faith—a faith with structure—and the fact that I could no longer follow the faith of my childhood. He looked at me patiently and said, "You talk like a Protestant. Why not explore the Protestants?" I lamented the fact that as a Catholic, I did not know where to begin. He then suggested I might like a man named Claypool at

Crescent Hill Baptist Church. I thought about his suggestion and then put it away as too difficult or not for me. I didn't know which.

Now that suggestion came into focus. I sat and thought about it. Maybe today was the day to act on it. I got up and found a city map. Where was the place anyhow?

I located the church on the map and plotted my way. The house-cleaning was done, so I could start out on my search. What did I have to lose? I got into my car. The rain was coming down steadily. The day matched my mood. I drove through unfamiliar streets and neighborhoods and wondered what I would do if I found or failed to find my goal. There was always the gun to go back to. I turned onto Bayly Avenue. Where was I going? For the past years I had read everything I could find in philosophy and theology to clarify my thinking. I had taken required courses and those not required in college in an effort to find answers to a faith that continued to elude me. Where was I headed now? What could this trip give me when all my previous efforts had failed so miserably? Somehow I felt that if I studied and worked hard enough, I would find the answers. Through my intellect I could surely find that God whom I needed so desperately.

Where was I going? I was at the corner of Bayly and Frankfort Avenue, and I needed to turn right. The rain was a downpour now. My windshield wipers were working hard to keep it clear. There was a library and then the church facing me. This must be it! It looked so large and cold. It turned me off—even frightened me.

I started to drive past when suddenly I saw the sign in front with printing on it. I might as well read it since I was there. I sat back in my car, shocked at what I was seeing: "Life Is Gift." I could hardly believe my eyes; and as I read I felt a surge of anger rise to challenge these words. Who says Life Is Gift? Mine certainly didn't seem so that day. Far from it. The time for the sermon? Eight-thirty. So life is gift! I'd see about that. I hit the accelerator and headed for home, my thoughts whirling.

On February 8, 1970, I got up at 6:30, dressed, and drove to Howard Johnson's for breakfast and then on to Crescent Hill. I timidly entered the sanctuary and moved forward about twelve pews before hastening to sit down. This was new to me, and I felt extremely uncomfortable about the unfamiliarity surrounding me. But everyone seemed very friendly both among themselves and toward me. I relaxed and waited, totally unprepared for what I was to hear as this worship service moved on. As the minister began to speak I recognized that I was hearing no ordinary person, and I leaned forward to hear his words better.

I immediately became aware that the minister was speaking of a leukemic child, his own; and my empathy rose. His daughter had died a month ago, and he spoke of his responses, his alternatives. This man, torn by grief, had a message I could hear. He expressed my own views that God owes us some answers for some things in due time. But he pointed out that attempts at immediate simplistic answers would not work. He used the story of Abraham. The point to the story was that life is a gift, one to be handled with gratitude. The minister pointed out that gratitude doesn't do away with pain, but it puts some light around the darkness and gives strength to begin to move.

I left the church that morning in a daze. I was filled with a grief-stricken empathy for this man who had lost his daughter and with shame that I had only yesterday thought of ending my own life. What right had I to throw away the gift of life? All of this gave me much to think of during the following week, and my depression lifted enough to allow me to think and to want to hear Dr. Claypool speak again the following week.

I told my therapist of my overwhelming experience, and he encouraged me to return to Crescent Hill. My session with him that week explored the depth of my feelings to an expanded degree. I was able to discuss long and painfully repressed material. Doors to my psyche, long closed, seemed to have opened because of my

Sunday experience in the worship service.

Toward the end of the week I was becoming anxious, experiencing a letdown about my former visit to the church and feeling a need to drive to Crescent Hill to check the sermon topic and time of service. To my surprise the topic this Sunday was "Therefore Choose Life." Again I felt as though I were receiving a message meant specifically for me. I drove home thoughtfully, almost unbelievingly.

On Sunday I repeated my preparations and arrived at church, daring to go several pews closer to the front and patiently awaiting for the beginning of the service. This time I received several messages. One was that I might face up to my freedoms and past failures and turn "so that the future that is yet to be will not be repetitious of the past." Another was, "The future is yours, you subcontractor of an unfinished universe—choose life!" These words have never completely left me. True, there have been more times of depression; but these words have always returned in time to help me.

As I drove home that day I was deep in thought. I had heard something that made great sense to me. I decided to call the minister and tell him of my visits and the intense impact they were having upon my life. A stranger, I hesitated to intrude but felt a great need to communicate with him. I telephoned that evening and found myself graciously heard and invited to return to Crescent Hill and, in the future, to meet him. I did not realize it at the time, but this was the beginning of a meaningful friendship with Dr. Claypool and the Crescent Hill fellowship.

After that week I continued to return for services at Crescent Hill and formally introduced myself to its pastor. As I became more comfortable and interested in this church, I began to realize I was finding a faith described in philosophy and theology books, through the care, interest, and concern of a good pastor and beautiful congregation. As this feeling grew I made appointments for conferences with Dr. Claypool.

I had many questions and arguments to be answered. Some came out of earlier doubts and problems arising from my childhood faith and others from the existential depths of my depression. My teacher was well prepared to assist me in both areas. He certainly understood my depression. We seemed indeed to travel the same road at times, as he was caught up in an immense grief process. While we traveled that road and talked, my faith grew. The grace of which I had read and studied and for which I had worked began to be real to me.

I slowly began to realize that, contrary to all my old beliefs, grace was not something I had to earn, but rather a glorious reality I need only accept and lay claim to as my own. This was, I think, one of the most important times in my life. A hope in life, long dead to me, slowly began to come alive. To me that hope became an important part of the light at the end of my tunnel.

Near the end of March, at the conclusion of a series of intense conferences, I reached a decision to make a commitment to Christ with the support of this fellowship surrounding me. Alone I would have been frightened, but with this kind of support I found the courage I needed. I was baptized on May 10, 1970. It was a day I shall never forget.

At the same time, new paths were opening to me in therapy. New growth was occurring in a psychological sense. I was barely beginning to get to the root causes of my depression and to do the work required to bring positive changes into my life. I had determination and the help of an excellent therapist. Now I also had faith and a church family to help on the long, hard road ahead of me.

As I write of these events during that depression, I cannot help being aware of all the ghost memories that have risen around me.

I remember what it was like to awaken after a drugged-like sleep, anxious and in the midst of a panic, to feel the terror of being in a semidarkened room and wish, childlike, to go sit under a nearby friendly bush.

I remember what it was like to hear the sounds of people around me and feel cut off, to sense a deep need for contact with others, but to avoid it because of a basic mistrust of people.

I remember what it was like to want to beg for help and be afraid to speak out, to always have the need to achieve and never feel quite adequate after achieving, to experience lonely nights and days and early morning wakings, to be drugged and tired at work.

I remember what it was like to wish to have it over; to perceive my entire body slowed down, daring me to accomplish anything; to experience sunny days that were always overcast, rainy days that were unbearable.

I remember a time when all green appeared the same dark shade and blades of grass all appeared as one vast dark green blur.

I remember what it was like to wish to smile and feel the tears form instead, and to be lonely—lonely all the time.

Time has passed, but these thoughts and feelings still surface on occasion and must be dealt with. The difference now is that I have a support system, a church, many friends, family, a trusted therapist, and a faith in God to take me further on my way.

****

Dorothy Steedly is a psychiatric nurse working in a hospital in Louisville, Kentucky. Her bouts with depression have intensified and deepened her faith in Christ and her Christian community.

2

Divorce

Ann Crosby

I remember walking out in the road in my bathrobe. For the first time in my life I didn't give a thought to whether the neighbors were watching me or whether they might consider me weird. And for a person who had normally been afraid of the dark's real or imagined terrors, I felt absolutely no fear of anything. I didn't care whether I lived or died.

The pieces were all there. I just chose not to see them until they crashed around me. In one night, the puzzle took shape. In two agonizing weeks, I had made the decision to separate and divorce. In a month, I was living alone in the house I had recently shared. I had thought divorce happened to other people—people who drank, or ran around, or in some way deserved it. I saw myself as a person who had always tried hard, perhaps too hard, to be nice, acceptable, and accepted. What was I doing in a predicament like this? That first night when I began to understand what a shambles my marriage was, I was in a kind of emotional shock.

The memories of those days are still sharp. I had been what I thought then was a strong person—a noncrier. After three weeks of feeling myself crumble and dissolve daily, I wondered if I would cry like this for the rest of my life. I lost ten pounds that first week.

I couldn't eat. I had always loved food, but at that time the smell or sight or even the thought of food made me actively nauseated. I was sleeping three to four fitful hours a night. I usually didn't get to sleep until one or two in the morning and was wide awake again by five-thirty or six.

I, who had a history of being a dedicated and accomplished student, now let all my graduate school work go. I didn't care what kind of grades I made. I did manage to go to class, but mostly because it was a relief to leave the house and be distracted. The rest of the time I wandered around the house turning on almost all the lights to try to dispel my almost overwhelming sense of confusion. And it is the only time that I have routinely turned on the TV every time I walked in the front door. I couldn't tolerate silence because that was stark evidence that I was alone.

A week or two into this lonely hell, a great-aunt to whom I had always been close broke a hip. She needed me. In my shame I had told no one about my situation, so I had to pretend nothing had happened. I had to give to her when I felt crushed and broken myself. I must have already been in touch with the remnants of my earlier faith because I recall throwing my fists at the ceiling and yelling at God for his cruelty in pushing me so close to my breaking point. It was shortly after this that I reached out to God, family, and friends for help.

It was not unusual, given my background, that I would turn to God in my desperation. I had grown up with strong roots in a Southern Baptist tradition. Although my family was not there every time the church opened, my models could safely be called devout in their faith. I had grown up feeling more fear than love of God. I had taken what I had been taught to heart and tried hard to live up to all the rules. As a child I would even make solemn commitments some Sunday mornings not to let an evil thought into my head, only to find I had failed utterly within minutes, before I got out the church doors.

I had devoted my first twenty-one years to living up to all I felt my immediate family expected. I had struggled to get to the top of the heap at a competitive private school and by the end of high school had been accepted by Vassar College. I had held my own there but not without the anguish of feeling that I was barely adequate, a feeling I had had for many years—one which probably had its origin in my trying to be as good as or better than my brother, who was three years older and also an achiever.

In college I had backed off my religion somewhat—I began attending church irregularly, but felt guilty. So in my junior year I did an unchic thing at Vassar and was elected president of Christian Fellowship for the following year. This was partly to assuage my guilt, but mostly out of hostility to beat another woman whom I felt had intruded in a dating relationship I had. So much for my noble Christian spirit.

After college and especially after my marriage to a nonbeliever and a nonchurch attender, I stopped going to church altogether. I had met and, after three years of dating, married a man who many would think had everything. Through him I had many wonderful new experiences, traveling, eating exotic foods in fancy restaurants, and shopping in elegant stores. He also offered a lot of intellectual stimulation. It seemed that the big pieces of my life at least were falling into place relatively easily.

But after a major move from New York City to southern California and not being able to find a job I wanted in social work, my unhappiness with myself and my three-year-old marriage increased. After eight months of marital therapy, my husband volunteered to give up his job and, in the face of disapproval from both families, move back across the country so that I could attend graduate school. He got a job fairly soon after the move. And we bought a house. But I remember standing on the front lawn of that house in an upper-middle-class suburb, asking myself "Is this all there is to life?" and feeling quite depressed at the thought that I had so many of the ostensible gifts of life and still felt unfulfilled.

I had been in search of something—I didn't know what—

throughout my life. I first believed I could find it during college. With marriage and all the material advantages I had, I really felt I should have everything I needed but knew I didn't. As I have indicated, I began to find this mysterious quality by losing what felt like the bulk of my life through a separation followed by a divorce five months later.

It is a good thing that there is always the option to grow from pain because it feels as if most of my significant growth has at some point evolved out of pain. And so it was, as I turned with full consciousness of my desperation to God. I started with a shaky belief that God existed—a shred left from my childhood training, so much of which didn't seem to fit anymore. But I began within a month or so to feel God's caring as a few things began to work out for me.

The first thing that worked out was my finally getting, after weeks of wondering and waiting, the best possible social work field placement I could have had at that time. A professor at school to whom I had reached out in my pain brought the job to my attention. It was a small counseling agency whose staff consisted of a Southern Baptist seminary professor and several graduate students. Six months earlier I would have avoided this agency precisely because its staff consisted of ministers, but now its size and the personal attention from the other counselors were significant factors in my beginning to heal. It was the first of several caring communities I have enjoyed.

Another critical event was finding a church that felt right. I had decided to try church again because I was willing to try anything that might help. I had not felt tied to my Southern Baptist roots; but after visiting several churches of other denominations, I found Crescent Hill Baptist Church. Crescent Hill didn't require that I accept a specified ideology in order to worship with them. The tone the minister set was one of striving to be honest with God and oneself. He quite accurately portrayed the church as a community of people who were seeking to live as if their faith mattered. I was challenged by the freedom to interpret God for myself and moved by his warmth. I did not get involved in the church for a year or so, but I did enjoy worship services. I never knew I could enjoy church before that. So often when I felt desperate and alone, the sermon would providentially speak to me exactly at my point of need. I felt God cared and was reaching out to me.

Much as I had, in my shame, dreaded telling my family of my decision to divorce, I found them understandably troubled, but loyal and giving. Friends also were thoughtful and supportive. The professor to whom I had turned helped me through the crisis and assisted me into getting into psychotherapy.

As time passed, other important things continued to work out. After months of looking and feeling about ready to give up, I found an apartment by posting a request at church, something I would never have thought of on my own. As I began to heal and regain my strength over the months, I returned to doing my schoolwork and graduated with honors. I was hired part-time in the same counseling agency in which I had completed my graduate field work. So I stayed in this valuable, caring community through the transition period of moving and looking for a full-time job. I also began dating a very special man; and although the relationship was not to last, it was an answer to my prayers and provided all the reassurance and intensity I wanted and needed then.

About a year after my separation, I learned I had gotten the full-time job in the inner-city hospital that I wanted. The same professor who had helped me earlier suggested that I check with a former student, who worked at that hospital, about any openings. There just happened to be a job being created. I waited and agonized for almost four months before learning I had been selected. This job in the outpatient psychiatric clinic was a challenge and a joy. The group I worked with became another solid caring community, as has the group I now work with at a pastoral counseling center.

These events may not seem related to God, but to me they were coincidences that I could not explain as pure chance—a friend's suggestion that led to my first apartment; a chance meeting with a well-known pastoral counselor which may have helped in my getting the hospital job; and that first interview question which happened to be "Do you consider yourself to be a Christian?" To me it was more than chance that my religion seemed to be the connection among so many constructive things working out in my life.

Sometime during this period I decided to take more initiative in developing my religious views. To my surprise, I began to see that what I was learning in psychotherapy went hand in hand with biblical teachings, as I was coming to understand them. I began to develop my own values. For example, I took the emphasis on honesty with others that I had learned as a child one step further. I now wanted to be honest about my feelings with God and myself. My old definition of a Christian as one who must do good deeds began to give way to that of a person who gives and loves freely.

I also decided that if I was going to have a good relationship with God, I needed to invest some time in that relationship. So I made a vow to read a chapter a night in the Bible. In doing this I began to see that the Bible contained "biographies" of other human beings, who—in spite of the fact that they are now considered as biblical heroes and were at times models in their faith—had pulled some incredible boners, some of which seemed worse than mine. I was getting significant help in coming to this understanding from a former minister at Crescent Hill, John Claypool. Through his sermons, which I received by mail, I began to see God as acting from a radical philosophy of living, forgiving, and accepting others, and not a God whom I need fear.

I followed my nightly Bible chapter with a time of contemplation and prayer. It began as a time to think through my day— things that I liked, nice things others had done or that I had done, what I had done but wished I had done some other way, and what, if anything, I needed to do in order to feel at peace about something that was still bothering me. I also remembered my great intentions of the night before, many of which had seemed to disappear into the thin night air before I ever woke up.

As I began to believe that God accepted me as I was, I also began to accept myself. I realized that the challenge was not to attempt to be perfect, or even to change overnight—rather, to keep on working and not to give up. It was a lifelong process, not time-limited as I had once thought. Before, I would often say to myself and others, "If I can just get this done, then I will be OK." Although it was easy for me to think of all the things that I wanted but didn't have, I also became aware of some valuable gifts that I had but frequently took for granted: life itself, my health, a stable family, caring friends, and a multitude of positive and challenging experiences.

It was clear to me by now that my reaching out to God was far more than crisis intervention. I had by this point built a faith which at times felt as strong and secure as a steel cable, and at other times somehow just out of reach. But I knew from experience that even if I was temporarily out of touch, God existed and cared and was involved in this world. My past was, and is, my evidence that I am not alone. I believe God has reached out to me through people and events. When I begin to doubt now, I think of some of the things I have shared with you. I remember walking through a shadow-filled valley and coming out to laugh again. I can face the future with hope.

My faith also helps me with my impatience. I like to dream about how I want life to be. I want my dreams to be like magical seeds which are planted one day, and sprout and bloom immediately. My faith helps me to accept the fact that things do not happen this way in real life.

A prime example of this struggle for me was my expectation that I would remarry within two to three years of my divorce. I have dated and tried to talk myself into falling in love with some who wanted me. I also have wept over others for whom I was not the right person. I have watched my ex-husband remarry within my expected time span and have given engagement parties for close friends. But, six years later, I have not yet found a man who has been the one for me. It has also been agonizing to watch my best childbearing years pass. At times I have felt so lonely and sorry for myself that I have wanted to die. I have called on my faith to bring me through these periods.

I comfort myself by recalling that although the Lord has provided amply in the past, it has rarely been within my time frame. John Claypool's sermons again have helped me to see that God's ways and God's timing are not mine, but are infinitely wiser than my own. Important events in my life may not occur exactly when or how I want them, but I have faith that my life will unfold in ways that are even better than I have imagined.

The result of all these events and insights was to bring me to a point of feeling that I was becoming a person I liked and respected. At times I feel very solid and stable. I believe I would never have gotten to this stage without the stress and pain which offered me the opportunity to grow as a person and a Christian. But I still struggle to understand the role of faith in my daily life.

As I look back over the time since I reached out to God, I see two broad stages that I have come through, and one in which I am still working. The first I call my silver platter theory. In essence it states that if I try hard enough to be a good person, God will provide everything; that all I need is enough faith; that if I believe enough and pray fervently, I will get whatever I need. Translated into today's lingo, this means "hope like mad" for miracles. I used this philosophy to rationalize a certain amount of passivity. I put myself in a very dependent, helpless stance and prided myself on humbly accepting disappointments.

The second stage occurred after a period of several years. As I felt stronger, I wanted to be more responsible for making good things happen. I was willing to take more risks to develop my personal resources; I stopped investing so much energy in squirming out of opportunities to grow. My prayer changed from "God, give me" to "God, guide me because I'm in gear." I went overboard, however, and soon found myself feeling depressed and overwhelmed. I realized that I had begun to think that my success was entirely my responsibility. I had come to view God as a benevolent bystander. My initial energetic will to take action turned into a massive burden and ultimately brought me to my knees again.

I am working now on finding a balance between the two extremes of expecting God to work miracles and assuming that I can do everything. I believe I can and need to do whatever I can in a given situation to make good things happen, but I am also acutely aware that there are real limits to what I effect, especially when other people are involved. I want to take responsibility for doing my part but also to depend on God's caring and willingness to be involved.

As you can tell, I am not at an end-point. I now accept my life as a process. I do acknowledge that I have grown tremendously since the night the pieces crashed around me. Since that time, I have felt greater pain than I ever knew existed. I have also experienced a peace and joy I had never felt before. I have been pleased with my professional growth and with my ability to handle the financial and social pressures of living alone. On the other hand, I also have a strong sense that there are areas in my life which still need developing further.

I have, however, found that previously undefined something for which I was searching. It is the peace of feeling acceptable to God and myself, and it is an acceptance which does not depend on external accomplishments. I don't have it all the time, but I know it's possible.

My pilgrimage over these last six years to this point of feeling at peace with myself has been so closely intertwined with my growth in faith and understanding of God that I cannot separate the two. I do know that the most important blessings I received along the way were God's forgiveness, mercy, love, and acceptance, which I experienced through events and the caring acts of other people. My greatest challenge now is to share these same gifts with others.

****

Ann Crosby is a clinical social worker who counsels individuals and married couples going through difficult times in their lives. She is active in her church and does volunteer work in her community in Louisville, Kentucky.

3

Death of a Husband

Betty Taylor Cook

What could be more depressing than a hospital admitting room on Christmas Day? Cold. Empty. Devastating. Our family waited, trying to find a laugh to cover the fear we felt. Cecil, my husband, was to be tested for possible lung cancer. I kept saying, sometimes aloud, sometimes to myself, "Just a precaution; he's too healthy for this to be serious." These thoughts, like the beads of a rosary, kept crossing my mind.

The patient was admitted and the tests began. The results left no doubt. There was a growth and it had to be removed. Surgery took place the last day of the year, a day past our twenty-seventh wedding anniversary. The year 1968 had begun with such promise for us. Cecil's promotion as vice-president of his company and a move to a new and beautiful home in a different city made me feel secure and happy. I was to learn again a lesson that I should have mastered long ago. There is no guaranteed security or happiness apart from the security of faith in our Heavenly Father.

The surgery was "successful" in that the cancer was removed; the lymph glands around the vocal cords were excised, and radiation was scheduled. It all seemed like a very bad dream. I found myself going through all of the motions of being a good Christian. I was strong and brave. Keeping my tears to myself, I covered very well the anger I felt—not toward God, but toward Cecil. Why had he continued to smoke in the face of mounting evidence linking smoking and lung cancer? As the days passed my anger changed to compassion and love. Cecil, who had been my strength through our lives together, now had become so vulnerable and so in need of strength from me. I learned that the best prayer is one for courage to meet life's crises. I learned that I am never utterly alone and abandoned, although I have to battle these two feelings constantly. Words from Isaiah were of comfort to me, "When you pass through deep waters, I will be with you; your troubles will not overwhelm you." The picture of passing through and not staying in deep waters was of great encouragement to me. To see an end is a blessing.

Spring brought beauty in new life all around and in our family as we welcomed our first grandchild, Matthew Mitchell Cook. We returned to normalcy in our lives. We did the necessary chores to "set our house in order." We made new wills and set up a new trust agreement which was a necessity in any case with a move to a different state. We had always tried to live in a stance that indicated we knew this life was not permanent. This knowledge served as a grounding for the time when death seemed a very real possibility.

Summer found us busy taking up *new* jobs in our church and learning *new* skills in our lives. Cecil took a course in speed reading, and I took a course for women who had been out of the job market and wanted to return. We watched men land on the moon and were thrilled by this achievement. But I was disturbed that so much was so easily spent on space exploration while so little was spent on cancer research.

Cecil had always had the joy of life which made everything seem like fun. Now this spark was gone from his personality, and death seemed to hang over our spirits. We tried to go about our daily lives as if the "invader" had not come into our home. Our five sons were grown, with the exception of our youngest, who was a junior in high school. Our oldest son was working on the west coast; our second son was in his last year at Union Seminary in New York; our third son was serving as a conscientious objector in a hospital in New England; and our fourth son was in the Peace Corps in Sierre Leone, West Africa. We found enjoyment in their lives and interests. But it was difficult for the family to be so far away from each other. There is strength in being together.

We read all we could about cancer and nourished our hopes with cases like Arthur Godfrey and John Wayne. They had survived lung cancer for many years. The following spring Cecil's cancer had spread, and there was involvement of his liver. He was hospitalized and my days were spent with him. We were as optimistic as we dared to be, but we were working against tremendous odds. We talked about my future alone, and we both knew in our heart of hearts that this was a certainty.

The last day of Cecil's life is a painful memory. I had stayed with him until visiting hours were over. As I left I told him, "I love you and I'll see you in the morning." I asked the nurses to notify me at any time, day or night, if there was a change. I would have stayed all night if he had been in a private room.

The next morning when I reached Cecil's room, I noticed a sign on the door. "Please check with the desk before entering Mr. Cook's room." I knew the moment I saw the sign that he was gone. I checked with the nurse and she went in and came out immediately. He had just died. I went in and saw him propped up in bed, eyes open, hands gently resting on his lap. He did not look as though death had been a struggle; it seemed only that he had quietly left this house that had become such a miserable dwelling for him. I closed his eyes, sat beside him, and held his hands. I was thankful that he had been released from so much misery.

Gathering up his few small belongings, I put them in his suitcase and started to leave. But a nurse and an intern took me aside to a small conference room and began asking factual questions about Cecil for hospital records. I'm sure this was necessary, but at the time it seemed an intrusion. I made my way down the hall. The elevator seemed so foreign, and I wanted to shout to the people: "Something terribly sad has happened to me."

It was a lonely walk as I crossed the familiar parking lot to the empty car. One should never take this walk alone. It seemed so unfair that after all of these months with Cecil, he died alone. It still seems so to me after all this time. I drove home on that beautiful morning; and though I had known Cecil's death was imminent, I still felt numb.

I went through the final activities with a studied peace and quietness. I had lived with death as an intruding presence for a year and a half. Death was a release from the prison that held the bright and happy spirit of Cecil Cook.

The days following his death were filled with the minutiae of legal obligations. It was necessary, I am sure, but what a lot of paperwork and activity! Our wills were in order, and this simplified the settling of the estate. My days were filled with meetings with lawyers and appraisers. Our home had to be appraised by three people, despite the fact that it was mine by a survivor's right. I felt both put upon and grateful for all of the people who guided me through the maze of chores that had to be done.

Early on I had a call from the Internal Revenue Service which filled me with apprehension. I knew I was not guilty of tax evasion, but the feeling was akin to being called into the principal's office. Armed with all of my records I made my way to the IRS office. Even finding the office and a parking place was difficult. What a delightful surprise awaited me! The agent I saw was businesslike, kind, and helpful. He was a Christian and was satisfied that we had really given what we claimed.

Knowing that our home was the last one Cecil and I had shared, I nevertheless put our dream house on the market. I had always read that one should wait a year before making any decision to change residence. After a year passed, I decided to return to Louisville, Kentucky, where we had lived for many years.

Buying a home alone is a responsibility, but also a challenge. It was a help to have realtor friends to sell my house and to help me relocate. Having to scale down was wise but not enjoyable. My selection pleased me, and the house I bought really suited my own personality better than any house I've ever lived in. I was encouraged by my ability to make a change which was not only wise but acceptable to my spirit.

The next decision I faced was employment. I knew it would be better for me physically, mentally, and financially to work. Realistically, I knew I was in for a difficult time. I had tried to find a job before returning to Louisville. I thought I was tough enough to face rejection, but it taxed my self-worth. I had been out of the job market for thirty years, and being a homemaker and a volunteer worker counted for little in marketable skills. I had taken several courses in library science, a refresher course in typing, and a class on writing resumés. My search led nowhere. The most affirmation I received was from the director of a kindergarten who said, "We almost hired you!"

Upon my return to Louisville, I was offered two jobs. One was with the University of Louisville Medical School library, the other with a book shop. I chose the latter because I needed to be with people. It was a stimulating job. I loved being around all of the new books and bringing buyer and book together in a perfect mating.

I worked in the book shop three years before taking a job with the American Printing House for the Blind. I presently serve as receptionist and tour coordinator there. We have visitors from all over the world. I take pleasure in meeting each one.

Employment has enabled me to travel. Being alone has a few compensations, one being the ability to act upon impulse. For instance, one day driving home from my work, I decided I would apply for a passport. This set in motion a joy that has filled my life with the pleasure of seeing new places. The four trips I have made to Europe have given me three different pleasures: the joy of anticipation, the beauty of realization, and the retrospective pleasure of reliving the trip. Trips to the southwest and Mexico, to the northwest and Canada, and to New England have made my life glow. The beauty, the sights, the mental stimulation, and the history surrounding each one excite me. There is always another place to visit and another horizon to explore.

The thought of a second marriage filled my mind during the first year of my widowhood. I was terribly lonely. I am sure if I had met the right person at that time, my answer might have been yes. The longer the time I've had to "go it alone," the more reluctant I would be to surrender independence. This is an option I keep open but would consider carefully.

My church fills an important place in my life. I have taught a class of young women, and together we have worked through many of the problems today's women face. Our church decided to elect women deacons, and I was among the first three. To be set apart by ordination for service is a sobering experience. It was one of the high points in my Christian pilgrimage. I have also had the awesome experience of serving on the pulpit committee, a responsibility of far-reaching proportions.

During all these changes my family has been encouraging. They have given me love and support, and they have had unswerving confidence in my ability to meet life's demands. Their confidence in my independence is a blessing, but at times I want to be cared for.

I have enjoyed seeing grandchildren grow and develop and regret the fact that their grandfather missed all the fun of being the special person a grandfather is in the life of a little child. I am so sorry he never met Sarah Taylor Cook, the first Cook girl in three generations. How he would have loved her! He would have been foolish over our twins, Taylor and Andrew. It is sad that he only barely met two little baby boys, Matthew and Dorland. I am sorry he didn't get to know Ben and Jon and Bill's lovely stepdaughter, Kris. I feel I must enjoy them twice as much for him.

I have experienced widowhood with many mixed emotions. I feel at times like the flip side of a good recording, just there to fill up the space. Sometimes I feel crippled by the loss of a part of me not seen by the world. In the final analysis I feel that life is a gift from a loving Father who wants me to live it well and with joy. A lack of joy in the events of each day is a supreme waste. We have been created to live and to take the events over which we have no control and weave them into a tapestry. This tapestry of our lives is made up of bright and vivid colors, as well as some which are muted and dark. All are woven together to make a pattern of beauty.

My walk is still not entirely free of shadows; but I continue my forward motion. The shadows are less deep and the darkness far less penetrating. I am aware of companions along the way who have shared in the shadowed paths. Together we walk with Christ, our elder brother and Savior. He has known the deepest darkness and has come through it. His victory promises that the darkness can be the beginning of light.

****

Betty Cook has been a pastor's wife, Sunday School teacher, and deacon in her Christian ministry. Her five sons and daughters-in-law, as well as her fellow church members, give testimony to her innovative and courageous Christian spirit. She lives in Louisville, Kentucky.

Women on Pilgrimage Through Change

4

Professional Therapy
Dottie Graves Dinwiddie

"I don't care what you do as long as you remember that the children come first."

"But Bill, they can't *always* come first. Sometimes I have to think about myself."

I couldn't believe those words had come out of my mouth. Me? The same Dottie who felt that the epitome of happiness was being the good mother, who had dreamed all my life of having babies, nursing them, nurturing them? They were still toddlers—and I was saying that at times my needs came before theirs? It frightened me so much that I ran out of the room, lip quivering, wondering what was happening to me. All those stirrings within me during the previous months were beginning to surface, and I didn't know what to do with them.

The decade between ages twenty and thirty had been too full and too fast. Graduation from college, followed quickly by the death of a close friend, the dissolution of a long-term high school romance, graduate school, marriage, two babies, our first home, settling into a career: so many "external" events, but not much time to sort out what was going on inside me. I had grown up in a world where family and church reinforced the model of women taking care of everyone else and being everything to everybody.

Setting limits for myself and defining my own identity rather than letting family, church, job, or society do it for me had never occurred to me. Also, dealing with feelings—particularly anger, pain, or disappointment—had been something I had never learned to do. Good Christians were not supposed to get angry or think of themselves first.

The day after my revelation to my husband I had to stop and take stock of my situation. I was thirty years old, in good health, in a marriage that had been rocky but holding together, happy in my work and enjoying my children. Somehow, though, this didn't add up to that idyllic picture of life I had in childhood. I felt pressured, always trying to get one more thing done, depressed at times, chronically tired, and generally uneasy about myself. Where was all this going? Why? What difference did it make anyway?

For years I had considered getting professional help but had been too "busy"—or, perhaps more honestly, too scared to risk it. Having chosen a career where I was constantly working with people who had emotional problems, I was well aware of the resources available to me. Even though I frequently referred others for counseling, it was a whole different matter to be seeking help for myself. A doctor whose judgment I trusted referred me to a psychiatrist about whom I knew nothing. Patients had frequently described to me how difficult it was for them to make that first call or visit to a counselor. I thought I understood their anxiety until I was in the same place myself. In some ways, perhaps one of the most difficult aspects of therapy is the process of making the decision to get help, making the appointment, and then keeping it.

As the psychiatrist said in our first session, I did not have the usual "ticket of admission" for therapy. I was eating well, sleeping fine, functioning well on my job, and basically happy in my relationships. I didn't hate my parents or run around on my husband. Somehow, though, something was missing, and I wanted to know what it was. Thus began a process that I thought would take two or three months. I was in therapy for two years on a weekly basis. It has been several years since I terminated therapy, and the changes are still taking place.

One of my greatest concerns during therapy was that I would become too dependent on my psychiatrist. Sometimes I worried that he would kick me out if I wasn't a model patient or if I let him know how angry I was with him about something. Perhaps I learned something about God's acceptance as he worked through those fears with me. I don't know if my experience in therapy was typical or not. Sometimes I wonder what would have happened had I not had a therapist who was a committed Christian, highly skilled, compassionate, and yet firm with me. I strongly believe that God works through people and events and that my experience in therapy was truly a journey toward wholeness. Here are some of the important things I learned about myself during that journey.

I discovered that it is not a sign of weakness or a reflection on my faith to need to turn to someone other than God, a minister, or myself to work with me through the issues I was dealing with. On the contrary, my experience in therapy served to deepen my faith and helped me to grow spiritually and emotionally in a way no other life event had done. My therapist at times represented God, at other times my husband, my father, or even my mother. Through him I was able to work through conflicts with significant persons, confusion in relation to particular life experiences, and unrealistic expectations I had created for myself.

I found that I could not deal deeply with my emotions without there being a profound effect on my spiritual life. I went through a period of doubting, not being able to pray, questioning things that many people deal with in adolescence. I had never allowed myself to confront those issues. Throughout, two factors remained constant. One was my belief in a loving God. Everything else related to my inherited faith was too confusing to me. The other constant was my church family. There were times when I felt as if I didn't belong in a worship service, yet I felt a desperate need to be there. Just to worship with people I had known most of my life seemed very comforting. The predictability of the worship service: same time each week, same place, same quality of music, all gave me a sense of security during my "dark night of the soul" that no psychiatrist, pastoral counselor, or Sunday School teacher ever could. I thought that "things theological" would eventually make sense, that there would be answers I could live with permanently. What I discovered, though, was that the more I questioned, the more there was to question. Rather than being frustrated by this, I began to realize that this process was keeping me alive and growing as a Christian in what my Sunday School teacher called a "healthy state of tension."

One of the most significant discoveries I made about myself in therapy was that I did not have to perform to be accepted. Making good grades, dressing attractively, saying the right things, volunteering when I felt I ought to, had all been a part of my behavior. I felt that the only way I could maintain my place with family, friends, and colleagues was by being the best mother, student, daughter, or player of whatever role I happened to be in at the moment. I demanded perfection of myself, even though my family had never pressured me to perform to win their love. As my self-esteem grew I realized something seemingly simple, yet it had eluded me for thirty years. I was loved because of who I was, not because of how well I performed or lived up to expectations.

Another important awareness I gained was that I was a person of need as well as worth. My parents had instilled in me a solid sense of being a good, worthy person who was loved and appreciated. They had also instilled in all their children a fierce sense of independence. It was considered a sign of weakness to ask anyone to do for us anything that we could do for ourselves. As a result, I even had difficulty asking my husband to bring me a cup of tea. At a deeper level, I felt I couldn't ask for anyone's time, especially to help me with a problem I thought I should be able to handle myself. *I learned that taking and giving balance out and that both are part of the process of being authentic in relationships.* And one is not necessarily healthier or more Christian than the other.

Much of my identity had been caught up in being a superwoman version of a wife and mother. That meant a full-time job, teaching Sunday School, baking my own bread, giving quality time to my husband and children, volunteering for everything I thought I should be doing, and keeping the household running smoothly. *As my identity changed from wife and mother to person, I began to define myself rather than letting others determine who I would be and what I would do.* I could set limits for myself. I could say no. I didn't have to be a supermom. I could take time to nurture myself rather than caring only for everyone else. If that meant a weekend out of town with friends and without family, I soon learned we were all better off as a result. Rather than being selfish, I was able to give far more freely and genuinely when I returned because I had some emotional reserves to draw on.

Another important realization was that *I can be ultimately responsible for myself.* As a child, when things didn't work out, I would run to Daddy and he would "fix" it. Then as a teenager I sought out boyfriends to make me popular and help me through my adolescent crises. As a young adult, I began searching for a man to "complete" me or to take care of me. If things didn't work out or I didn't know what to do, there was always someone else I could turn to. I was not accustomed to making final decisions and then being solely responsible for the outcome. In therapy, my psychiatrist wisely refused to take over for me or to be responsible for my decisions. I had to make those ultimate decisions. In the process, I learned that I need others for input, feedback, and support, but that I can trust my own judgment and intuition for the final decision.

I also learned that I am not half of a whole in my marriage. I did not have to have a husband or a child to make me a whole person. Coming to a sense of feeling complete within myself kept me from becoming frantic at the very core of my being if illness, death, or conflict threatened my relationships with people who were most important to me. There was a spiritual dimension to this sense of wholeness that came from a new understanding of how God is at work in my life.

Another major issue in therapy was that of control. *I had been in control of my emotions but did not feel in control of my life.* Things just "happened" to me. If I could allow myself to express my emotions more freely and also be more in control of events, my life could be healthier and more productive. In the family in which I grew up it seemed that the only acceptable emotion to share was happiness. Good Christians didn't get angry. It was a sign of weakness to cry. Fears and insecurities were feelings one kept to oneself. We rarely expressed affection openly with each other. *Once I began acknowledging my fears and my emotional needs, people began relating to me at a more intimate level.* I later learned that others had tended to put me on a pedestal. I was living up to the myth: "Dottie never hurts; Dottie is never confused." I had to begin to undo the myth, and in doing so started becoming more human, more vulnerable. In the process I started becoming more real to myself, to my family, and to my friends.

Another part of the control issue was my need to control or change other people. *As I came to feel more of a sense of control in my own life, I seemed to have less of a need to control others' lives.* I had also been spending a great deal of energy waiting for significant people in my life to become the kinds of persons I thought they should be. I finally realized that the more pressure I put on them to change, the less likely it was to happen. Also, the more anger I stored up because they were not the way I wanted them to be, the more distance came between us. I began asking myself how I could relate to a particular person the way he or she was rather than the way I thought he or she should be. I still find myself having difficulty with this one!

Sexuality had been a part of myself I had many hang-ups about.

As an adolescent I feared that every time I talked to a male there would be some kind of negative sexual connotation, that he would think I was flirting with him. I feared that if I cared deeply for another female, people would think I was a homosexual. As I became more comfortable with myself sexually, as I got rid of some fears and inhibitions, *I found that I could have emotionally intimate relationships with persons in addition to my husband.* It was a relief to realize that I could trust my motives in these relationships. It took the pressure off the marriage to meet all my emotional needs and made for a far healthier balance for my husband and me. It is satisfying to have intense relationships with a variety of persons and not feel that I am denying my sexuality or my capacity for emotional intimacy with these friends or family. *I found that sexuality is not something one "does" in the bedroom. It is a healthy part of my identity in all my relationships.*

I also finally internalized the fact that *emotional intimacy with others is worth the risk, even with no guarantees about the future.* After the death of my college roommate I had unconsciously decided not to risk needing someone or caring so deeply for another person. I never wanted to experience the pain of a sudden loss again. I had heard the term "unresolved grief" for years but didn't really know what it meant until I finally had to deal with the pain of the loss of my friend. In a crazy sort of way, holding onto my grief was my way of holding onto her. Somehow I felt that if I let go of those memories, I would lose all I had left of her. What I hadn't realized was how that grief had kept me from enjoying life with the intensity and joy I had felt prior to her death. My psychiatrist gently but firmly worked with me to let go of the inhibiting, crippling part of the grief so that I could risk being vulnerable again.

Where have I come with all this? It has been several years since my experience in therapy, and I am almost forty years old. If my twenties composed a decade of "externals," my thirties a period of inner search, perhaps my forties can be a period of pulling the two—the what and the why—together in a healthier manner.

Even though it was an emotionally draining experience, in a paradoxical way I found the process of therapy to be energizing and at times exciting. It was not a one hour per week occurrence; the issues were constantly on my mind. I did not come to the realizations outlined here without confusion, fear, and, at times, pain. I still struggle with some of the conflicts and feelings. I learned that the goal of therapy was not to solve all my problems. I am a healthier, more authentic person as a result of my experience, though, and I find that I am coping with the problems I face in a more constructive, confident, and realistic manner.

None of what I have shared here could have occurred had I not had the support of a loving family, a church that knows what pain and struggle are all about, friends who care deeply for me, and a patient psychiatrist. For all of this and for a God who gave me this kind of Christian community in which to grow, I will always be grateful.

****

Dottie Dinwiddie is a professional counselor in private practice in Louisville, Kentucky. She is a deacon in her church, president of her Sunday School class, and plays the violin in her church orchestra. She leads workshops and speaks on subjects relating to developing one's full potential. Her two children, Laura and Joseph, give her added reason to develop that potential.

5

Career Resumption
Carolyn DeArmond Blevins

A ringing telephone provokes varied reactions. Anticipation. Excitement. Curiosity. Irritation. For me on that September day in 1976 it was irritation. Again I was interrupted. And this inter-ruption became permanent. For the caller had a problem and hoped I might be the solution. Carson-Newman College was inun-dated with freshman students and extra classes were needed. Would I teach a religion course for them?

Part of me wanted to say, "I'd love to. I've dreamed of teaching at the college level." An even larger part of me wanted to say, "Have you taken leave of your senses? Don't you know how in-competent I am? No. I can't." In a stupor, I said, "Yes." As I hung up the telephone my struggle began.

As I look back at my return to a career outside the home, the problems of making that change have centered around two con-cerns: self-esteem and time. During seventeen years of full-time homemaking I had discovered a lot of pluses and minuses in the role of housewife. I enjoyed the package of tasks called homemak-ing. And though I suffered periodic bouts of feeling unappreci-ated, generally I felt good about my housekeeping and childrear-ing skills. Those years of satisfaction and fulfillment gave me a reservoir of positive feelings about my value and skills in managing a home.

Experience and common sense taught me as wife and mother to juggle the use of my time according to the priorities of the moment. Family, of course, was a top priority. I appreciated the luxury of staying home to enjoy each of the four children as she or he arrived in our family. Fortunately, the "Mommy, look what I can do!" moments outnumbered the "Who threw spaghetti on the curtains?" moments.

One of the cherished assets of being a stay-at-home mother was freedom. I could work like crazy for a day or so and then spend a day relaxing with a gripping book, a dear friend, or a jigsaw puzzle. I was free to arrange personal gifts of time for myself.

Returning to a career was a terrific jolt to these enviable advantages of being home most of the day. Learning to do another job well and to manage with less time at home meant I had to learn new skills and new ways of coping. I came out of a comfortable cocoon into uncertainty. But that uncertain world of college teaching attracted and challenged me. I had to reach out for it.

I love to teach! A brief stint at public school teaching, Sunday School classes, Vacation Bible School, and mission studies had given me ample opportunity to discover that I enjoyed teaching. Preparing to teach always taught me more than I taught others. Teaching at the college level was a dream come true, but. . . . It had been sixteen years since I finished seminary and I was rusty! Besides, college students knew too much. How could I teach them? But. . . .

Here was an open door I did not want to shut. Shortly after I hung up the phone, panic set in. Next Tuesday at 1:30 I had to stand before a college class as their teacher! Rather quickly I concluded that saying yes was clear evidence I'd lost touch with reality. Since quitting is a foreign word to me, I had to put my anxiety to constructive use.

My greatest fear was displaying my ignorance before college students. My husband, Bill, is a college professor. He assured me over and over that on my worst day I knew more about the Bible than most college students. He insisted there was much I could teach them. He just didn't know how little I remembered from my seminary classes!

The next few days were a whirlwind of frantic preparation. On Tuesday I walked into class faking poise and confidence and feeling panic and fright. It was really going to be embarrassing when the students proved they knew more than I. That would show Bill how ignorant I really was. I survived the class and the students survived me! However, I was sure it was just a matter of time until the day my hidden incompetence would be exposed.

Each class session became increasingly easier. My perpetual anxiety kept me surrounded by books and writing pads. By the end of the year my self-esteem was returning. Several factors contributed to that return. First, I made it through the school year! If only I had known in September that I would. Second, I began to believe in myself. Bill was right. I did know more than I thought. Third, the student evaluations of that spring rated my teaching as very effective. That verdict was a bonus I needed. Fourth, I was offered a full-time teaching position for the next school year. All around me I was discovering support and confidence. The confidence others had in me prodded me to live up to their expectations and to develop my own sense of worth.

But the battle wasn't over. I now had an opportunity to do something I enjoyed and get paid for it. I was ecstatic! And frightened again. As full-time teacher I'd have more classes the next year. There were not enough hours in the day for me to prepare for four classes the same way I'd studied for one course. Now failure on a large scale was entirely possible.

The year was spent working hard and staying one-half step ahead of the students. I was continually learning but still had feelings of inadequacy. That was four years ago, and I still struggle with feelings of incompetency. In the meantime, I have concluded that I am an effective teacher who still doesn't know enough about her subject. But that's a healthy tension, for it motivates me to keep preparing and learning constantly.

While my perception of myself as a competent teacher was rising, my long-held self-image as a good homemaker was plummeting like a free-falling skydiver. In my attempt to survive the first months in the classroom, I gave the homemaking tasks scant attention. I began to feel guilty about what I wasn't accomplishing at home.

Guilt was a feeling I knew well. As a homemaker it had plagued me or motivated me. I discovered that career mothers have double doses of it. I wanted to do well in my tasks at the college. And I wanted to maintain my standard of being wife, mother, daughter, housekeeper, active church member, and community worker. When my standards exceeded my body's capacity to perform and my mind's ability to cope, some changes became mandatory.

Gradually, and with painful adjustments of attitude, I concluded that my self-esteem couldn't be based on a superwoman fantasy. That model would lead to perpetual work and probably increased guilt, not to mention an exhausted me. Self-esteem as a homemaker with a career had to be firmly anchored in reality. Once more priorities and common sense began to shape my personal expectations.

Guilt was not in my genes, but in my learning. It was nurture, not nature. If I had learned to feel guilty, I could learn not to feel it. Consequently I began to categorize my guilt feelings. Some guilt I began to ignore. So the kitchen floor wasn't mopped often. My sense of worth did not hinge on spotless floors. Some guilt motivated me. When several weeks had passed since I visited a shut-in friend, guilt caused me to go by her house for a delightful visit. My "ought to" voices became useful vehicles for nudging many of my "want to's" to the top of my priorities. That kind of guilt was helpful in transforming intentions into accomplishments. Other guilt I began to accept. About four o'clock in the afternoon an uncomfortable feeling began to grow on me. The children were home from school and I wasn't there. I still don't like that idea, but

I am learning to live with it.

Wrestling with various kinds of guilt is a part of living. Guilt is like an umbrella. Occasionally I walk under it, but I don't live under it. In the best interest of myself and those who live with me, I refuse to live under a canopy of guilt.

My struggle with self-esteem continues. I've come a long way since the day of the phone call. But my journey is far from over.

In the first stages of my new career I was enveloped in a fog of finding a new sense of worth. All other difficulties were secondary to the question, "Can I do the job?" As I walked out of that fog into a clearer vision of my new routine, I discovered an even larger problem. Time.

Time governs my daily activities in much the same way as stop signs govern my driving. Just as I gain momentum, it is halted by a signal which seems to scream "Time!" There just isn't enough of it. That fact of life I learned early in my new career.

Each evening our family members returned home. No one had been there during the day to tidy the house, wash the clothes, cook the supper, or run family errands. Tasks that I used to spread out over the day and do somewhat thoroughly now had to be abbreviated, shared, or neglected. We chose to do a little of each.

One of my first decisions was a significant one for me. I decided in favor of sanity. Insanity has never appealed to me, especially my own. So for sanity's sake, I came to three conclusions: (1) I would learn to live with lower housekeeping standards. (2) I would not plan to accomplish many household chores at night, since I frequently needed to bring schoolwork home. (3) My time would be used for the highest priority of the moment.

Living with lower housekeeping standards is my most persistent frustration. I know my frustration is reaching a peak when I get the feeling that the food I've prepared wants to be excused from our table. Or when I can almost hear the coffee table begging to be dusted.

The quality of our meals has suffered embarrassingly. When the children complain, I know it isn't just my imagination. Cooking is not so bad if I have taken time to plan ahead. But planning tomorrow or next week's meals is often what gets squeezed out of today's schedule. The worst part of my day is often when I walk out of my office about five o'clock wondering, "What in the world am I going to have for supper?" You can bet that is the night the children will have legitimate reasons to complain.

Bill knows this struggle and frequently says, "Why don't we go out to eat tonight?" I am most vulnerable to that question! At 5 PM I have very little willpower to refuse any proposed solution to the problem of the next meal. But the dilemma doesn't end there. If we go out, I am greatly relieved that I don't have to worry about the meal. Yet guilt overwhelms me, for we are spending extra money because I didn't take time to plan ahead. Sometimes I rationalize eating out by convincing myself we should enjoy some bonuses from my additional salary. But meals remain a persistent problem.

A clean house has been another sacrificial lamb of my new career. A spotless house was never worth the effort for me. Once or twice I have had a very clean house, but it was always when no one was home but me! Quickly I had decided that apple-pie order was sterile. I wanted a home where people lived rather than an intensive-care ward. So I had adopted moderate standards of cleanliness. Since I started teaching even those standards have taken a sharp nosedive because I don't have as much time.

The choice was clear. Every member of the family could do part of the work, even though it wasn't done as well as I had done it. Or I could do all of it myself and do it right. Obviously the joys of housekeeping had to be shared. The children would have settled for less joy! They already had household duties, and Bill pitched in as needed. Now everyone had to take on additional tasks. To be quite candid, the carpets are not as clean as I'd like, the bathrooms suffer hit-and-miss attacks, the perma-press clothes sometimes come out of the dryer with a prune look—and all that bothers me!

But not enough to stay up until 2 AM every night to do all of it myself. So I live uncomfortably with lower standards.

Returning to a career meant not only days away from home, but also taking work home at night. So time at home isn't always time to spend with family. Sometimes enjoyable family experiences or household tasks take a backseat to grading papers or preparing a lecture.

Reduced time at home also means a perpetual juggling of priorities. I am not as free to do everything with the family as I used to be. Before I worked outside the home we frequently picnicked, hiked, or biked in the mountains. It's harder now to work those pleasures in. And we miss them. I can't be homeroom mother as easily, an experience I miss with no pain except that it was so special to our children. When Bill speaks in various places, I don't go with him as often as I once did. We don't entertain as much.

Most days I give my attention to what is most urgent that day. My priorities vary quite a bit: preparing a dinner for guests, planning a lecture for tomorrow, going to Alan's band concert, working on a church committee, going out for an evening with Bill, writing a Sunday School lesson. Career, husband, children, church, and leisure take turns rising to the top of my list of priorities. The problem of priorities is no different than it was when I was a full-time homemaker. It just has new wrinkles in it.

Less time at home also means that those personal moments I used to arrange for myself are now rare treasures. I miss having time to curl up in front of a fire with a best-selling novel, sew a dress for Kym, or bake cookies for Suzanne, our daughter in college.

Time. Every day it's a problem. As a jigsaw puzzle addict, I think of each week as a new challenge of fitting bits of time together. I'm still in the process of learning how the pieces of time best fit.

So it's been a hurdle to leave full-time homemaking for a full-time career. Change is usually painful for me, but out of that pain I frequently reap personal growth. This change has been no different. The adjustments have been many; the growth has been abundant.

Recognizing my own potential isn't always easy for me. God has given me more abilities than I want to admit. Bill often sees those gifts long before I do. He continually stretches me to reach potentials I am sure do not exist. Without his strong support I would not have made the career leap. Bill is helping me learn to be a good steward of the skills God entrusted to me.

Returning to a career has taught me new truths about God. In my preparation for classes I am confronted over and over with new insights about God and faith. It's exciting to have the opportunity to teach students the Bible and their Christian heritage. I am able to lead some students to a richer faith. That experience enriches my own.

One of the most exciting and awesome discoveries I've made is that many of my limitations are not God-imposed but self-imposed. The "I can't" voice within me is mine. As I have stepped out in fear and faith, I've discovered that "I can" because God has gifted me. "I can't" is my attempt to limit what God can do. "I can" is my faith that if God has equipped me, I must try.

The benefits of a new career have not been entirely personal. Our family has profited literally and figuratively from my employment. The additional income has relieved Bill of the total pressure of funding our family. Our children enjoy the privilege of buying brand-name jeans and eating out more often. We can spend two weeks at the beach rather than one. The new income has relaxed the penny-pinching pressures to some extent at our house.

Even more significant is the benefit to our children. We have tried to teach them increasing self-reliance. When I began to work outside the home, that process accelerated rapidly. Each of them has learned some basic living skills such as vacuuming, washing clothes, simple cooking, cleaning house, and making their own hair-cutting appointments. Art, our older son, readily acknowledges, "It's been good for us. We've learned to be more independent."

All of us have experienced the pain and potential of adjustment. My struggle with self-esteem and time will continue, for they are closely entwined. The pressure of time frequently reduces my feeling of competency. The children continue to grumble about their chores. But I will continue to stretch my intellect and my faith. We will continue to become more independent persons. And we will celebrate what each of us is becoming.

Long hours of preparation, always walking into class wishing I were better prepared, the support of my husband, the encouragement of our children, the neglect of many household tasks, and the abandonment of some personal pleasures characterized that first year of my career. They have characterized every year since. The interruption in our lives is permanent. It is stretching all of us to find new potential.

****

Carolyn Blevins teaches in the Religion Department at Carson-Newman College, Jefferson City, Tennessee. She writes curriculum materials for The Sunday School Board of the Southern Baptist Convention and has authored a book entitled *Christ: Style for Discipleship* for Convention Press. She and her husband, Bill, who also teaches religion, have two college-age and two younger children.

6

Return to College

June Holland McEwen

The line moved slowly, winding through the lobby and around the gymnasium floor. In one hand I clutched registration materials and with the other held firmly onto my four-year-old son, Jeffrey. The two of us were at odds with the bright, chattering crowd of eighteen-year-olds all around. Mother and son slowly made their way from station to station amidst the ordered chaos of college registration.

Freshman registration at the University of Chattanooga in 1964 was not the usual place for a thirty-four-year-old housewife, pastor's wife, and mother of two. The wave of adults going back to college had barely begun. Jeff and I were as conspicuous as blue jeans in a ballroom; I was conscious of our differentness while Jeff delighted in the novelty and activity. Melanie, aged eight, was happily at play with friends, while Jack was making his round of hospital visits. And here I was trying to become a college freshman sixteen years after completing high school!

About the time of Jeff's birth and coinciding with my twenty-ninth birthday, I began to have intense feelings that there must be more to life than the repetitiveness and the routines that I had established for myself and my family. These feelings were vague and difficult to articulate—even to myself—but they were strong

58

and compelling enough to overshadow the steady accomplishments that Jack and I were experiencing in our lives. Jack had completed his seminary degree at Southwestern Baptist Theological Seminary and was continuing to grow in competency as pastor and leader. Somehow his successes no longer gave *me* any sense of personal achievement. This mishmash of emotions made for occasions of frequent conversations between us about how to make our lives count, how to better serve God, how to be more effective in the church, and how I could gain a more contented state of mind. In the climate of the day and in the context of our place in a church environment, it seemed wrong-headed of me to want to do something on my own, something separate and distinct from the work of my husband. Jack tried to understand my dilemma, but he left our talks very puzzled and discouraged.

After I married at nineteen, the focus of my life and the end of all my activities was Jack: his career, his education, his achievements, and his work. It was taken for granted by those around us, by him, and by me that his accomplishments were mine also. My role was to stand to one side or stand behind to help him, applaud his successes, to cope with his failures, and to spend my energies and talent in his work. Neither of us (nor our friends) questioned the rightness of this system.

Why, then, did I begin to question a way of life that seemed to work and to have the sanction of society and the church? Partly it was the times—women across the country in every strata of American life were beginning to question, some rather stridently, the way things were. I had worked after school during high school and had managed my own money since I was fifteen. Being the older girl in a family of six, I had long been a leader and decision maker, a person who was responsible for myself and for others. In high school I was a leader in my class, accustomed to speaking out and making decisions.

My mind-set was one of self-reliance and independence. Little wonder that after ten years of marriage and of submerging myself in someone else—regardless of how worthy—my troubled feelings began to emerge. So here I was: twenty-nine, my husband with a diploma, a bachelor's degree, and a divinity degree; my two children bright, healthy, and enjoying growing up, while I kept wondering what was happening to me. Why was I so confused and discontented?

Who was I, other than someone's wife and someone's mother? What was wrong with me that these two honorable roles were not satisfying? Slowly a long-buried dream of a college degree was resurrected as a way to answer these questions. Education seemed to offer a way to discover a place for me. I felt I might become a person in my own right with concrete accomplishments that were truly and uniquely mine.

Armed with high hopes, I set out to earn a college degree. At the same time I intended to fulfill completely my role as mother, wife, homemaker, and community volunteer. It was not by accident that Melanie was happily placed at a friend's and that Jeff had gone with me to registration. No mere babysitter for my children while I embarked on my venture into self-fulfillment! As an aspiring supermom, I expected to meet all obligations and to perform superbly in every area of my life. My intention was to maintain number one priority and superior performance in every aspect of my life.

How did I arrive at such unrealistic expectations of myself? Growing up in a large East Tennessee family in the thirties meant sharing work at an early age. All six children did assigned chores without question. Times were hard for everyone; and with our large family, things were extremely difficult. My parents made it clear that we were expected to do well in school, do our work at home, keep personally clean, live honestly, and obey our elders.

Doing well at school was no problem for me; I loved school. My clearest memories are of good teachers. Miss Irene, my second grade teacher, read dramatically the adventures of Mrs. Miniver and William Greenhill to her bright-eyed listeners. Mrs. Cox expected excellence from all her fifth grade pupils. Miss Capps and Miss Scarabrough were junior high teachers with the ability to motivate and to inspire teenagers. I responded eagerly to them all.

After moving to Knoxville in 1943, I discovered Lawson-McGhee Public Library. This opened up the world of books to me and gave me the chance to become acquainted with the works of Alcott, Dickens, Scott, and many, many others. I gobbled up biography, fiction, and history with no plan; I started by selecting books that looked good to the eye or felt good to the hand.

At this same time, a Baptist church reached out to me and my family. I responded to a visitor's printed invitation left on our doorknob inviting us to ride a bus to church the next Sunday. Being from a small town, I found the bus ride an exciting opportunity and an adventure not to be missed. The large, friendly, enthusiastic congregation enfolded me in its fellowship. I was soon baptized into membership, enlisted in helping with a class of five-year-olds, involved in the youth program, and included in a supportive and caring family of Christians. It changed my life.

My high school years in Knoxville were marked by immersion in the life of the church, working after school, and doing well academically. Following graduation I saved my summer earnings at Ellis and Ernest Drug Store and took a passenger train to Fort Worth, Texas, to enroll in a Bible school. I intended to serve God by serving my fellowman as a foreign missionary. This vocation was changed when Jack and I met and married.

The first years of our marriage were filled with his being in school, working as a minister of youth, as assistant pastor, and then as pastor of a tiny church in Hillsboro, Texas. During all these moves and assignments from 1949 to 1952, I worked as receptionist, clerk, or secretary as well as in Sunday School, Vacation Bible School, and other church tasks, ranging from typing the bulletin to keeping the nursery.

While in Hillsboro, Jack and I enrolled at Baylor University.

After one quarter I returned to the work force while he continued his studies, pastoring, and driving a school bus. We joined forces to get his education and to build a church.

An exciting opportunity came in 1952 when he was called to be pastor of the Baptist church in Daisy, Tennessee. I continued my work as a volunteer pastor's assistant in this larger, rural church while Jack entered the University of Chattanooga to complete a bachelor's degree. When I was twenty-five, Melanie was born, adding the dimension of motherhood to my life. Melanie was eighteen months old when we loaded everything we owned in a rented trailer and moved to Fort Worth for Jack to study for the divinity degree at Southwestern Seminary. I worked hard as nursery coordinator and as the general assistant to my student-pastor husband. The church and its organizations flourished.

Jeff was born when Melanie was four. After graduation from seminary, Jack accepted the call of Northside Church in Chattanooga to serve as their pastor. Back in Tennessee and serving a lively and challenging city church, I plunged into church work and added PTA activities to my schedule when Melanie entered first grade. By now the frantic round of church, home, and community involvement submerged the strong feelings and longings I had experienced when Jeff was born. Periodically I would stop, consider, and face up briefly to the undercurrents of wishing for something more—something ineffable and unnamed—some deep need that was not being met. Quickly getting involved in more activity, I managed to brush these thoughts and feelings aside.

Jack encouraged me to try again to realize the old dream of a college education. He insisted that I enroll at the University of Chattanooga and take at least one course to see if that would provide some of the satisfaction for which I longed. Deciding to take this one course, I realized that I faced one surprising obstacle. I was afraid of competing with the younger students! After all, I had been out of school for so long; I had worked behind the scenes of church; and I had done only routine clerical jobs during the first two years of marriage. I had no particular competency and no specific skills. I was older; I was a housewife. How could I presume success as a college student?

To my surprise and delight, I was not only a good student—I excelled! It was exhilarating to learn, to research, to write, to attend lectures, to fill up blue books. I reveled in the heretofore-unexplored areas of philosophy, history, political science, literature, music, and art. I enjoyed it all. It added zest to all my waking hours.

Along with the fulfillment I found by entering the academic world, I was determined to maintain a full schedule of teaching Sunday School, working in Church Training, attending WMU, and participating in all phases of church life. I was careful to maintain a schedule for dinners, visits, hospital calls, and other facets of a busy pastor's activities.

Melanie and Jeffrey enjoyed seeing Mother as student. As first and fourth graders, they often drilled me with flash cards to help with French vocabulary. In return, I pushed myself to read to them, serve as Brownie leader, room mother, PTA committee member and president, cookie baker, party giver, and other jobs of a busy mother.

I placed impossible expectations on myself to do it all; the church work, the PTA work, the housework, the family time. I attempted to do everything as well as if each area was the only area. How did one find time to be a wife in the midst of all this? How about keeping alive relationships with parents and other relatives? My sense of setting priorities was nonexistent. Why such frantic and frenetic activity? These questions were never allowed to surface; they were pushed aside in favor of more activity.

I thought this busy life would prove my worth. In ever-mounting activity I wrote for the university student newspaper, participated in the University Scholars, and became president of Mortar Board while continuing an active role at my children's school and my husband's church.

All this "busyness" took its toll on Jack. He quietly went his way and did his work. He played with the children, helped with baths and bedtimes, and continued to meet a demanding schedule. We were both professing and practicing workaholics. The stresses were felt in various ways: excruciating back pain, recurring migraines, occasional insomnia.

I wish I could describe here how we solved all this by sitting down and facing the stresses and strains, analyzing causes, and planning a joint attack. Not so. We simply endured. We were committed to each other, to marriage, to our children, and to the church. The Lord supplied strength: physical, emotional, and spiritual, almost in spite of our hardheadedness. Looking back over the four years of my college experience I see that they were years of unremitting stress. I regret that I did not manage the experience in a more positive and constructive manner. I should have learned earlier to set limits for myself. I made the years harder than they needed to be.

The cost of reaching my personal goals was made incredibly higher by my foolishly trying to do everything and to do it to perfection. However, in looking back over a difficult yet exciting time in my life, I can see many lessons learned. There is no growth without pain. Couples should set mutual goals and work toward them with support and understanding for each other. A family will do better when they schedule together times of work, play, leisure, and other activities. Patience, forgiveness, understanding, and true communication are indispensable virtues for families. When the family is willing to help each individual become all that that person is capable of becoming, joy is enlarged and personal fulfillment becomes a truly mutual celebration. My pilgrimage to discovery of the academic life and to obtaining a college degree was a rocky road. Today as I continue to grow as a woman, as a person, and as a Christian I try to benefit from the many lessons learned both in the classroom and in my family circle. I remain a pilgrim on a journey of growth, struggle, and discovery.

****

June McEwen was an English teacher and pastor's wife in Chattanooga, Tennessee, before moving to Louisville, Kentucky, with her husband, Jack, in 1980. She writes grants for The Southern Baptist Theological Seminary; Jack is dean of the School of Religious Education at the seminary. June writes for *Royal Service* and other Baptist publications.

7

Change of Career

Kay Wilson Shurden

I sat across from the kind face and soothing voice of Dr. Wayne Oates of the University of Louisville School of Medicine. My husband and I were taking him to lunch at Jim Porter's Restaurant. I waited patiently for the right moment to ask my not-so-subtle questions about a possible change of career from teaching to counseling.

A flood of unanswered questions swelled behind my calm exterior: "Why didn't I make this decision to become a counselor three years ago, when we first moved to Louisville? Now the timing is all wrong! Can we afford for me to go through a two-year training period just when the first of our three stairstep children is going to college? Certification is indefinite, and clients are nonexistent. Am I sure I can 'make it' in this new venture? Is forty-two too old to begin again? What if I fail?"

Leaving these uneasy questions, my mind fell back to thoughts of my secure groove of teaching. In one form or other, to one age or other, teaching had always been my career. My first teaching job was in New Orleans: English and Reading, grades seven and eight, while my husband worked on a divinity degree at the Baptist seminary there. Then came five years scattered over various grades of elementary school. Each time one of our three children was born, I gave up a classroom and invariably found myself teaching a different grade when I returned the following year. I had lesson plans and teaching materials for every grade from third through eighth! Then my husband's doctorate was completed in Church History, and we moved to a full-time pastorate.

Ruston, Louisiana, was a university town; and ours was a university church. There I began work on a master's degree in English. It had always been my favorite subject, especially literature. I figured I could read some of the world's greatest works if I could get someone to assign them to me. And I was right! Two years later I had read myself into an M.A., just as our youngest child finished kindergarten.

Before the degree was actually in my hands, we moved to the hills of East Tennessee to a small liberal arts college, Carson-Newman. Buddy, my husband, joined the Religion Department faculty, and I was asked to supervise and teach student teachers for the Education Department. Most of the students under my supervision were teaching English, so I used my past classroom experience and my newly acquired degree.

Teaching college students was a new and exciting challenge, but it left me a bit shaky! With my family's support and encouragement, I began taking a few courses at the University of Tennessee nearby. As my hours mounted, I decided to take a year's study leave from Carson-Newman and complete the residency requirements for an Ed.D., a doctorate in Education. My official residence was still at home with my family, but my mind resided at UT! The following year I wrote a dissertation on "The Image of Women in Adolescent Literature" and received my degree and a promotion at the college. I was set for life! Or so I thought.

Periodically, Buddy got offers to move to other positions. When the offer came from The Southern Baptist Theological Seminary in Louisville, Kentucky, we were pleased, but not persuaded. We were interested, but reluctant. Our schedules were coordinated and relatively slow. Life was uncomplicated. Why change?

But I kept my foot in the door lest he close it. My thinking went something like this: Buddy would be stimulated professionally by the teaching position at the seminary, and surely I would be able to find many teaching jobs in a place the size of Louisville. Besides, I had some thoughts that teaching might not always be my career choice. Louisville might offer some options. However, for the present I wanted to teach. On a preliminary visit to Louisville I was interviewed and practically hired on the spot for a teaching position similar to the one I had at Carson-Newman. We decided to move.

That position did not come through for me. I never really knew what happened. The chairman of the department promised to get in touch with me right away, but no word came. Finally I called and got an evasive reply. Six weeks later I received a two-sentence letter that the "position in English Education has been filled." In characteristic fashion, I wondered what I had done wrong.

Trying to put that one negative experience out of my mind, I applied to the other colleges and universities in the area. Nothing except part-time teaching was available. On the hope that something part-time might lead to something full-time, I took two positions: one in freshman and sophomore English at Indiana University Southeast, and the second, a night course called "New Horizons for Women" at Bellarmine College. The latter proved to be both a prod and an omen about my own future.

The women who registered for "New Horizons" ranged in age from twenty-three to fifty-eight. All were at decision places in their lives. One was a waitress who wanted a more meaningful and better-paying job. Another, the mother of school-age children, had been out of the job market for ten years and wanted some courage before tackling the world of work. A woman in her fifties faced an empty nest and wanted part-time work around interesting people. On and on the situations went. All the women wanted from their work what I wanted: meaning, fulfillment, and good pay for their time!

Other less obvious problems faced them. They were concerned

about the effect their work might have on their marriages, or their children, or their commitment to church responsibilities. Counseling them about their individual situations and stresses, I discovered again something that had challenged me in teaching at every age level. The *content* of what I taught wasn't nearly as important as the *interpretation* of the content and its *application* to life. At Carson-Newman I had enjoyed helping student teachers move from theory to practice, from learning *about* education to doing it in the classroom. I was thrilled with watching their personal and professional growth. At Bellarmine I was excited about working with women who assessed their skills and interests, studied the job market, and then set about to make these decisions fit into their lives. I knew my interest came from my own struggle to do what they were doing.

At the end of our first year in Louisville, I still had no permanent teaching position. I felt pressure from several directions. First, I felt like a professional failure. I could find no permanent position. No one wanted me except as an adjunct or a fill-in for overflow students. That didn't do much for my ego!

Besides the pressure of my own feelings, I felt the pressure of finances. Child number two was beginning her senior year in high school. We were about to begin the double-tuition period, which would have no let up for four years or longer. If I ever needed to be financially productive, it was now!

Suddenly, three full-time teaching positions opened up almost simultaneously. One was in a business college, another in a community college, and the third at a county high school thirty miles away. The first two offered more status for my wounded ego, but they also required me to teach evening classes. That really didn't appeal to me. If the kids and Buddy were away every day and I was away at night, when would we be together? Besides, our time with the kids was almost gone.

I decided to take the high school position. I knew I'd miss the flexible schedule which is a part of college teaching. But I rallied around the fact that at Carson-Newman I taught teachers how to teach high school English. Surely I could do it easily!

I couldn't have been more wrong! High school teachers are some of the world's greatest heroes. And I taught with some of the best. But I didn't number myself among them. The first year I suffered but survived. The second year was better, but the thing that really kept my battery charged was the course I continued to teach once a week at Bellarmine. I found the high school inflexible, the students (especially sophomores) unresponsive, the discipline downright deplorable—and worst of all, I found myself absolutely uninspiring. This last feeling, that I wasn't doing a good job, really got me down. My first year left me so drained emotionally that I had to remain a second year to prove I was no quitter.

Of course, there were bright moments. Especially the second year. Colleagues were sympathetic and helpful to one who was now teaching in the "real world." Many students, some who called me "Doc," became friends and sought counsel about personal matters as well as advice on college and graduate school. Tyrone, one of my favorite sophomores, was sure I was teaching him college English. There was so much he didn't understand!

One of the highest honors and biggest surprises of my life came the year after I left Shelby County High School. The senior class voted to invite me to speak at their baccalaureate. I couldn't have been more surprised! They may not have meant it this way, but I have interpreted their invitation to mean that feeling failure and actually failing may be two different things. Apparently I was failing myself more than I was failing them.

The spring of my second year of high school teaching found me at Jim Porter's Restaurant with Buddy and Dr. Oates. My "joy quotient" was only slightly above zero. Blurry feelings about counseling as a new career were focusing inside me. Thoughts about the next twenty years of my life and how I would spend them demanded attention. What should I do? Could Dr. Oates offer another option?

He did. And then I did. He offered a postdoctoral residency, and I entered a two-year supervised training period in counseling under his direction. My two years in community psychiatry at University Hospital could fill a book in itself! Now I am in a private counseling practice and have had time to reflect on the patchwork quilt of all my education and positions. How do they relate to what I'm doing now? And why did I feel it necessary to change careers at age forty-two?

Several main currents of thought and feeling rush forward to demand expression. The first one concerns the relation between counseling and my previous career in teaching. The feeling is this: Nothing has been wasted! My elementary school, junior high, high school, college, and adult teaching experiences gave me the broadest base possible for counseling with people of all ages. From the sixteen-year-old boy who's unpopular at school to the couple in their sixties facing the challenges of growing old together—I've met them before at Shelby County High or at Bellarmine College. Their developmental tasks and their styles of learning are a part of my past experience. They're unique people, but I've taught many people like them. I draw on the bank of these experiences daily.

I also draw daily from the skills I developed in teaching third grade math or sophomore English. Like the teacher, the counselor helps the learner find the way. Rather than handing out the answers, the effective teacher shows the learner how to ask questions, discover resources, focus on goals, and choose from among many alternatives the one best suited for him or her. The process is the same in counseling. The skill I developed twenty years ago teaching fourth grade in New Orleans applies in my counseling office today in Louisville. Nothing was wasted!

I've spoken of my many past careers as patches in a patchwork quilt. And I think of my new career in counseling as the quilt as a whole, made up of all the patches. I think the thread which holds them together is my sense of ministry.

I strongly believe in the ministry of the laity. As a Christian I believe that I have gifts given to me by God. One of my responsibilities, as well as one of my joys, is to develop and use my gifts. The place and manner of using my gifts may vary, but part of my discipleship consists of ministering to others through using my gifts. Each patch in my patchwork quilt is an expression of my ministry at a given period of my life. And God has threaded them together so that some use can be made of them now.

Counseling as ministry is real to me. People who turn to a counselor are at life's low places. I feel I've been given the gift of walking with them through those low places and onto higher ground. For some reason they may have been blocked, but in counseling they feel the freedom to continue their pilgrimage. My own pilgrimage is given a boost by helping others continue their journey. That is the nature of ministry!

Another feeling which demands expression here is gratitude. I'm grateful for the privilege of changing careers when I felt the need to. Most men and many single women do not have this option. Many times, for the sake of security and paying the bills, they must stay with a job they no longer enjoy. Also, many married women may not realize that they can actually find a job which gives meaning as well as financial dividends. A reluctance to change as well as a fear of failure may hold them back. One purpose of my story is to offer encouragement to consider a career as a form of ministry. This means that gifts will be used as fully as possible. One index to deciding whether to change careers is to evaluate how many gifts each career uses. The more the better!

My career change has also helped me to be grateful for closed doors. When some doors close, we begin trying to open others. At least that's the way it was for me. For example, I am now grateful that the job offer when we first moved to Louisville never materialized. If I had been offered a permanent college position at a good salary, I probably would never have had the courage to venture into my present career. That big, painful door of rejection, slammed in my face, forced me to look around and within.

I am even grateful for my last two soul-searching years of high school teaching. They spurred me on in earnest to find a career which fit me better in this period of my life. Though painful at the time, they helped me move to a more joyful and realistic place of service.

I do not think a career change is what everyone needs. A job doesn't have a magic quality which makes all things right. But my experience was one of moving from feelings of frustration and rejection to feelings of worth and fulfillment. My career has become my ministry. This makes my pilgrimage worth the pain and uncertainty of change.

****

Kay Shurden likes writing, teaching, and speaking, as well as the counseling she describes in her chapter. She and her husband, Walter, dean of the School of Theology at The Southern Baptist Theological Seminary, Louisville, Kentucky, have an "empty nest" since Sherry, Paula, and Walt left. She serves as a deacon and Sunday School teacher and chairs the Education Committee in her church.

Women on Pilgrimage Through Choice

8

Personhood
Eleanor Wilson Nutt

I married a five-talent man who was industriously turning into a ten-talent man. I thought I possessed only one talent. I had buried it so deeply I could not find it. Therein lay the equation I was to learn to solve as an adult. The talent I finally dug up was enough to build on, to build with. To my amazement my talent search has continued, and I am finding personal resources I never dreamed I had.

Memphis, Tennessee, was the place of my high school graduation. The year was 1955. My whole life had centered around the church. To me God was the Great Judge. I had heard little of a loving or forgiving God. Fear was the basis of my faith. I lived in a black and white world, believing that my commitment to God was exemplified by the list of things I did not do.

I was a very fearful person who had neither excelled nor failed. That was because I never had the courage to try anything. While in junior high school I wanted to be a cheerleader, but I was afraid of entering the competition. Even in high school, I felt afraid. For a few months I was in a high school sorority; however, I dropped out because I did not know how to dance, and I was uncomfortable going to the parties. I made a bold statement that I was "giving up dancing," and my church applauded my decision. I felt safe.

My Christian beliefs mirrored my fears. Peace at any price was necessary. I believed that if I prayed and read my Bible daily and attended church every time the doors were open, I would be favored by God. I believed that since God caused both good and bad happenings in life, I simply needed to be his puppet. My life was very simple. My thoughts regarding my future were also simple. I had been taught that women were meant to care for others. I never fantasized anything but being a wife and mother. And I really wanted to be a preacher's wife.

Baylor University in Waco, Texas, seemed like a good place to find a preacher. And I didn't even have to wait for the fall term to begin. In August, Grady Nutt came to my home church from Baylor to lead in a youth revival. He and I became a "number" immediately. I was so impressed that this Big-Man-on-Campus was interested in me. He was a junior and was involved in all the important activities at Baylor.

We dated constantly for two years before we married. During my student years at Baylor my only identity was that of being "Grady's girl." I did not participate in any activities on my own. He chose my classes, professors, friends, even my wardrobe. My life continued to be very simple. We were the ideal couple. When we married we took great pride in having never had an argument. It took me years to wise up enough to realize that this was possible only because we both agreed with him, both loved him.

In June of 1957 we "became one." My simple life soon became very complicated when I got pregnant the first month we were married. Picture, if you will, two immature people who did not know how to communicate, did not know how to handle money, and had not made any significant life plans. Things began to happen quickly in a haphazard manner.

Grady's first job as a minister was in Waco, Texas, where we stayed only eighteen months. When it was time to put down roots and perform a significant ministry, we were frightened by the task. We moved to another church. This time home was in Dallas, Texas.

We were in our second city and we had our second baby, all before our third wedding anniversary. Our marriage was constantly deteriorating. Our simple life continued to become more complex. I was distraught. I was praying, reading my Bible daily, taking my babies to church, doing everything I knew to do to please both God and Grady. I was dying inside, but I never spoke a word of my pain to anyone, least of all to Grady. He had a terrible temper and was very opinionated. I was afraid to disagree with him because I firmly believed that people who truly loved each other would not fight. Therefore, I withdrew from the "battle" and used tears as my weapon. Grady did not know how to handle my crying, but at least I was getting his attention.

In August of our third year we felt that we had to move again. This time we brought our two babies and our ailing marriage to Louisville, Kentucky. Grady enrolled at The Southern Baptist Theological Seminary, and again we were sure that a new situation would help us; but we were only putting bandages on our wounds. By now he and I were hardly even friends and we had two frightened, unhappy little boys.

Grady and I had learned early how to look like we were in control, how to pretend to have our lives in order. It had never crossed our minds that the church would be a place to go for help. Church was where Grady worked. Church was where we went to talk about how we were so blessed. Church was the last place where we thought tears would be understood.

We treaded water for another whole year before going under. On a Sunday afternoon after Grady had preached, our lives finally caved in. That day Grady said that divorce seemed to be the only way out for us. I was horrified: How could this be? I had done everything that I had been taught to do. My faith had no room for this kind of hurt. I felt that my life was a total loss. All that I had ever believed was going down the drain. I had no way to make a living. I knew that the children would be my responsibility. I did not even have a friend to call.

The next day I made the first courageous move of my life. I

called and made an appointment to see a marriage counselor. I had never known anyone who had received professional counseling and had no idea that any other seminary family had ever had a problem.

On my first visit I was totally honest with my counselor about the conditions of my life and my marriage. I expressed with words as well as tears my anger, hurts, and fears. This was the first time in my life that I had allowed myself to be honest about how I felt. The second time was one week later when I finally gathered enough courage to tell Grady that I had sought help. His first reaction was rage. He stormed out of our apartment, and I really never expected to see him again. Several hours later he returned a broken man, ready to receive help and open to do all that he could to help us build a new and real life together. Looking back at the depression and fear of those days, I now realize that the courage to seek help had to come from God.

As Grady and I began to receive counseling, our lives started to change. It was painful. It was slow. At times we wondered if we would ever get things together. It proved to be worth all the energy and much more. We didn't solve all our problems, but we did learn how to work together to meet our needs.

I made one dramatic discovery in my initial counseling session: When Grady fell in love with me, I was a person with a personality. During the past five years I had become an echo to him. I said what I thought he wanted me to say; I did what I thought he wanted me to do. I had to become a person again—with or without him.

Taking control of my life for the first time at age twenty-five was frightening. Most of my life I had measured my gifts and strengths against those of other persons. In my judgment, my gifts and strengths were inferior. I decided eventually to strike out on my own, without Grady's help, on a solo adventure. I wanted to see for sure if I had what it took to achieve a worthy goal that would be my attainment, my success, my accomplishment—not as

"Grady's girl," not as "Grady's wife," not as "Grady's better half."

I took a course to prepare me to be a professional model. This had been a childhood dream. Having finished the course, I modeled professionally for several years. I often copied designer fashions and sewed them for myself. I finally saw my home economic skills as gifts. Having a beautiful wardrobe that I could make well and look good in became important. For a while I was a slave to what was "in." I was intimidated by the people who seemed to me always to be dressed "right." In time I learned not to let someone else decide for me what I should learn to decide for myself. Modeling taught me a lot about good design, fabrics, style, and comfort. I have been able to assimilate this into my system. Now my physical appearance is a statement of who I am—not a disguise for life's masquerade ball.

Modeling began the process of my coming to feel good about my body. I came to realize that how I look greatly affects how I feel about myself. I know that I look better at a certain size and weight. I am willing to pay the price of diet and exercise to maintain that. I discovered that I can be an intelligent, thinking woman and the same time can enjoy being feminine.

My solo adventure carried me much further than being a professional model. I began to believe that I too had some gifts. My self-confidence steadily emerged. Growth was very slow, but each new venture helped me to try harder.

Twenty years later in Lubbock, Texas, while attending a workshop, I had an insight that made a great difference in how I see myself. Grady's gifts are *different* from mine, but they are not *better* than mine.

One of my best gifts is that of being a friend. I do this easily because I have a great need to have a few intimate friends. These friendships with both men and women are important to me and necessary for me. I am better able to understand my needs and my gifts when I have a few close friends who can mirror to me what they see in my life. Through these friendships I have come to have

82

a growing sense of security about my capacity for emotional intimacy.

With these people whom I love I can be who I am. I first shared this kind of friendship with a small group of people at the Crescent Hill Baptist Church in Louisville, Kentucky. With them I learned to celebrate my strengths and my joys as well as share my weaknesses and pain. Whatever is real to me is real to my friends. Through Grady and other friends I have come to believe in a loving God who also is forgiving. The priesthood of all believers has become real to me. At times I am the priest who shares out of my abundance; at other times, my friends are my priests.

I so clearly remember the painful days when I thought Christians were to be strong and not express suffering and anguish. How grateful I am that I now believe in a loving God who cares for me through my church and my friends. I never take the good gifts of friendship for granted.

When I am in control of my life, each new venture that I undertake gives me courage. In the early years and stages of our marriage, when I had no self-confidence, it was easy to assume that almost every other woman had more to offer Grady than I. This caused me to be overwhelmed repeatedly with feelings of jealousy.

As Grady and I began to learn to communicate, and as I began to discover my own sense of worth and personhood, I began to develop a growing sense of trust. Over the years I have found that my ability to trust Grady has grown in direct proportion to my ability to feel good about myself. I am now his partner, not his shadow. We are equal. I am not his better half.

I was able to choose not to be employed outside of our home. Caring for the children and keeping house were things that I loved to do. Grady was traveling in his work, and I felt that the boys needed the stability of my being at home. Most of the time I did not feel trapped and enjoyed parenting. However, quite frankly, there were ages and stages when I would have sold the whole operation—cheap!

During those ages and stages when we had difficulty with our boys I felt personally responsible. After all, I was staying at home giving parenting my best energies. I tried for several years to rear two perfect sons. By the grace of God and with Grady's help, I came to realize that all I needed to do was give parenting my best shot. After that, I had no reason to feel guilty. I backed off and also came to realize that good parenting meant that I would steadily work myself right out of a job. My best gift to our sons was to help them become independent, responsible people.

My independent, responsible people grew up and left home. The empty nest has brought joys that I never dreamed of. It didn't take long for me to realize that twenty years of up-close parenting had been plenty for me. Now I was ready to take care of me. I could read my books without being interrupted. Grady and I could eat when we wanted to without waiting until after ball practice. We would have a house full of people on Friday night only if we invited them. There were seldom ever any sweat socks to wash. I have loved it all, and I love my adult sons in a richer and dearer way than ever before.

Grady and I have been working with young adults in our church for fifteen years. I have seen many of them struggle to break away from parents who can't let go. These young adults taught me how much they need their parents' blessing to leave home and need to be able to move into an adult-to-adult relationship with them.

To be able to relate to my sons as adults is one of the great joys of my life. As we relate to them with honesty and sensitivity, they respond with like kindnesses. Perry and Toby are people whom I would want to be my good friends even if they were not my sons. Like all of my close friends, they teach me and I teach them. We take seriously our family relationships. We all give to each other, and we can all receive from each other.

With my empty nest came many questions about how I would spend my time. I feel that I have been in control of my life for years, and I have been choosing exciting, creative things to do that keep me growing. I often meet new people who ask me what I do, and I am sometimes embarrassed when I have to respond that I do not work outside my home. I do not want to be thought of as one of the stereotyped women of suburbia who drinks coffee, watches soap operas, and gossips with the neighbors all day. When I was actively parenting, it was a bit easier to explain that I did not work outside my home. I do not know many other women who are in their mid-forties, who have no children at home, and who are not gainfully employed.

I still do not have an easy answer for the "What do you do?" question. I don't even have a familiar category to put it in. I do know one thing, however; I enjoy not being employed.

For the past two and one-half years I have served as a deacon in my church, with my deacon responsibility being pastoral care. During this time we have had only interim pastors. I am grateful that I have had time to make this my "job." I have learned much about my own abilities while at the same time directing many activities and programs that have been significant to my church. I am fortunate that I can choose where I shall become involved. With help from my friends, I am coming to the point of being able to believe that I am really OK, just as I am, without having a paying job. I am able to affirm my abilities as a minister, teacher, and student of life. I am no longer frightened by the unexplored horizons in my life. My close friends, ministers, and counselors have taught me that to be open to growth and change is to live life fully.

Grady and I have learned that marriage for us is best when as equals we relate out of strengths and not just our needs. From my young adult friends I have learned how to have a quality relationship with my adult sons. I have learned from my friend Ruth Highsmith that retired people, who are often confined to their homes, have beautiful gifts to give as well as burdens to bear. One special role model, Vera Peterson, has taught me that being the right kind of person, loving and caring for others, does not guarantee smooth sailing.

I salute the struggles of life: my own struggles, the struggles of others that I share as friend and sister. From these struggles I grow, I learn, I explore, I find my gifts.

****

Eleanor Nutt is a warm, creative, efficient, shrewd, and capable person. She leads the Pastoral Care Committee, serves as deacon, and teaches seminary couples in Sunday School at her church in Louisville, Kentucky. She speaks for groups, decorates, sews, and believes in friends. She and her husband, Grady, are ministers in many ways.

9

Dual Careers
Nancy Drown Allen

Grading final exams doesn't usually make me cry. As I graded my last set of American Literature exams that spring, however, I found that I could not choke back my emotions when I read the notes my students had written to me. "Good luck in Louisville— we'll miss you," one of them wrote. "I hope you like your new job," said another. Staring at the exams, my eyes filling with tears, I realized I was experiencing the most painful problem of having two careers within one family—moving when the other spouse is not ready.

I had just resigned my job as a part-time instructor at the University of Alabama, not to take some glamorous and better-paying job, but to look for *any* job that would help support our family. My husband, Mike, was going back to graduate school, and I had agreed to quit my job, move to Louisville, and help further his career. *His career.* The words repulsed me, seeming a direct contrast to my students' warm words.

Why had I agreed to such a stupid move, I wondered? I soon realized that I had done what so many women had done before me: I had assumed that my husband's career was more important than mine. Since Mike is a minister, I assumed that God had "called" Mike, but not me. But I had done my job well, I argued to myself. I had introduced students to the world of literature and self-expression through writing. I had seen sleepy eyes light up with the excitement of Faulkner's descriptions or Twain's humor. I had challenged, even angered them. And I had been a friend. I remembered the student who came to me because she was pregnant and didn't know where to turn. The middle-aged student whose daughter was on drugs. The young woman whose husband was an alcoholic. Surely God had intended for me to be there. *Someone* will shape them during those first college years, I reasoned. It might as well be *me*.

My own sense of purpose could not change the fact that I had agreed to this move many months earlier. I hoped that God would make some sense out of this unhappy situation. I even began to wish that my work in Louisville would somehow be better than my work in Alabama.

Searching for a job long distance is like trying to look up a Scripture verse in a Bible that has no numbers or book names. It is also depressing. My job search began seven months earlier, as I set up interviews with all the colleges in the Louisville area. Full-time jobs for college English teachers are rare these days, but I kept hoping. After all, God *did* part the Red Sea. During this time of lining up interviews I also looked into job possibilities at The Southern Baptist Theological Seminary, where my husband would be enrolled. I found that few people there seemed to take seriously a seminary wife having a career. A job was mandatory, but not a *career*. One man told me to forget finding a job in my field, that a secretarial position was all I could hope for. Not only did advice such as this depress me, but it also angered me. It gave me a determination that somehow I'd show them all. I just couldn't believe that God had helped me through the agony of graduate school and somehow didn't intend for me to use my training and my gifts. I had to figure out a way to keep teaching!

The frustration of job hunting while living four hundred miles away—with occasional trips to Louisville—was increased by the lack of understanding I received from those around me. Most people viewed my concern about finding a job as purely financial in nature; and, of course, that was true in part. But no one seemed to realize what teaching meant to me. No one recognized my sense of call.

I found that this uncertainty about a job had taken its toll, because I had many symptoms of clinical depression. After dragging through each day, I went to bed only to lie there sleepless for hours. Usually I cried in the bathroom while my family slept, and none of them ever knew the condition I was in. This crying usually left me exhausted enough to sleep for a few hours. I considered seeing a counselor at this point, but I felt that this depression was a direct result of my career upheaval. Deciding to endure, I hoped that the depression would disappear when I received my first paycheck.

My faith in God's hidden purpose got me through this depression. It also kept me determined to find a good job against all odds and against all the pessimistic warnings of friends and acquaintances. I became familiar with the yellow pages of the Louisville phone book, and soon my letters and resumés had been sent to everyone who might be even remotely interested in someone with my language skills. Meanwhile, both the University of Louisville and Indiana University Southeast had offered me part-time teaching jobs, so I had renewed hope.

Finally, I got several calls from Louisville. A horse magazine needed someone, but the pay was low. I was assured, however, that I'd be able to keep my part-time teaching jobs if I worked at the magazine, since this office operated on flexible time. Another offer came from an engineering consultant firm which used proofreaders. The pay there was considerably more than at the magazine, but the hours would probably preclude my teaching. After much thought, I chose the magazine job. I felt that this choice was a bit risky, but I kept remembering my sense of purpose in teaching.

Only later did I realize that I had lucked into the best of both worlds. I was in the perfect spot for an English major—publishing, writing, and teaching. Now, three years later, I write an article each month for the magazine, teach three English composition courses, and even take riding lessons, one of the benefits of my connection with the magazine. In short, these jobs have been more fulfilling than I could ever have hoped. Meanwhile, my husband is closer to getting his Ph.D. in Christian Ethics.

The crisis of giving up my job in Alabama has passed. But in its place remains the ongoing problem of two careers in one household. Of the two-career marriage, much has been written about the problems of housework, professional competitiveness, and children. But our problems seem to fall into one category: our stereotypical roles, which we have reversed at many points.

In addition to working from nine to four each day at the magazine, I teach composition two nights a week. Thus, I have one more career than I asked for. Naturally, this busy schedule produces the most common and often talked about problem of having two careers in one family, that of sharing responsibility. Fortunately for me, Mike is not threatened by housework. The first semester we were in Louisville he cooked dinner four nights a week. We did not eat TV dinners either! Mike discovered that he actually enjoyed cooking. He planned meals and delighted in inviting guests to sample his latest dish (many of which he invented). He also learned that vacuuming floors and ironing shirts can be done just as well by a man. I found out that I knew almost as much about my car as Mike did about his, and I have found a good place to get a tune-up, no longer having to bother Mike when my car isn't running smoothly. The key to successful sharing of responsibility is flexibility and willingness. We have never rigidly divided up duties, but we are both willing to fill in where needed.

With this practical division of chores, many people might think we have found the perfect solution to the two-career marriage. Many of the problems, however, are actually more deeply rooted than the worry of who will go to the grocery on Friday. These are problems that come from our listening to the howls of society around us. The simple fact is that *most* couples do *not* function the same way we do. And these couples are our friends. The result is that we both run into resentment, wonderment, and sometimes even jealousy from observers. These reactions of others are perhaps hardest to take and frequently make us respond to each other unkindly.

Our female friends always think Mike is wonderful because he "helps" me. The illogical assumption here is that the housework all belongs to me, so he is simply "helping" with my job. These same women rarely, if ever, see me as "helping" Mike by taking care of the car or dealing with the insurance agents or taking care of our finances. There is also the subtle implication that I am not as good a mother as they are, that I must not love my children in the same way they do since I have chosen to work outside the home. Sometimes our female friends even make an example out of Mike to their husbands: "Why can't you help me like Mike helps Nancy?" More than one husband has been known to respond to this insensitivity: "When you get a job like Nancy, I will."

Needless to say, this kind of reaction from friends is embarrassing and frustrating. I always feel slighted by women who think Mike's cooking baked apples makes him perfect, and Mike always feels slighted by men who insinuate that his cooking—while being substantially funded by a working wife—is less than manly. With more and more women entering the job market, there is a need for understanding among women who work inside the home and women who work outside the home. Each group carries some suspicion about the other, but respect for individual choices would benefit everyone.

Occasionally even teasing can be difficult to take. My mother (a working mother) laughed after suggesting to my children that they ask me to sew a patch on their jeans. "Oh, Grandmommy," they said, "Daddy will do it." Mike's brother commented that Mike would make someone "a good wife," to which his mother replied,

"He already has." And Mike once invited a friend to eat dinner with him and our children while I was teaching. He prepared one of his favorite meals: stuffed pork chops and fresh broccoli. Like most cooks, he waited for praise, only to find that the young man assumed that *I* had cooked the meal and left it in the oven before I went off to class! I laughed at this, but Mike was angry. Thus, while most working couples think division of housework will solve all the problems, they may find—as we have—that sometimes going against society's stereotypes can be painful.

Society's attitude toward working actually produces the problem of professional competition in the two-career marriage. We all want to be appreciated for what we do, whether it be teaching, driving a bus, or baking pork chops. When I feel unappreciated and not respected as a professional, I also feel angry at my husband, even though it is not his fault. This hostility stems from my anger at society's assumption that a man has a career while the woman has only a "job." I view myself as more than just a second source of income.

Continuing crises in a two-career marriage are always amplified by children. Most women who contemplate entering the job market shudder at the logistical problem of having children cared for all day. Our children, Matt and Eric, are in school all day, and they now come home to an empty house. Although there is a next-door neighbor who is always there if they need her, they usually entertain themselves for an hour before Mike and I arrive. Eric and Matt are what sociologists call "latch-key children" and what some mothers shake their heads at.

My children are not unhappy with this situation, but I feel guilty about it. I'm not sure why. I assumed that *all* children should come home to a smiling mother who opens the door for them (hence no need for a key hooked to their backpacks), presents them with a plate of freshly baked cookies (with real chocolate chips, no doubt), and discusses the traumas of their day. The truth is that my two children—and I suspect those of other people—come home tired, kick off their shoes, eat some store-bought cookies, and watch an hour of "Our Gang" before they want to talk to anyone. Only then do they seem ready to face the neighborhood gang with barbs and taunts and secret plans.

The children's routine sounds strangely like that of most adults, with their wanting to unwind after coming home from work. My worry, therefore, seems unfounded. Eric and Matt become more and more self-sufficient each day. It's not easy to admit that they can do fine without me for short periods. Even when I occasionally imagine all the horrors that could occur in my hour's absence, I realize that most of them could also occur if I were at home baking brownies. Dealing with Eric and Matt's independence and my guilt is only one more problem incurred from having a career of my own.

My other guilt comes from having a house that looks more like a garage in *Popular Mechanics* than a scene from *House Beautiful*. Even Mike and I working together can't keep it looking perfect all the time. I used to be embarrassed about this seeming failure on my part, but I'm beginning to recognize the practical limitations involved. Children constantly stream through the Allen house, and I'm convinced that they come into my kitchen to clean the leaves and dirt off their shoes before going home to their mothers' clean houses. My children claim that some mothers in our neighborhood won't let their children bring friends in; but Mike and I want our house to be a home for our children, so we have sacrificed perfection for fun. I still don't know how the Oreo cookie got in the vent in the bathroom, but I've been happier since my husband pointed out that our house is just as clean as many where the woman stays home all day.

If there are so many crises involved in having a career of my own, surely there must also be benefits. Perhaps the primary one is my sense of personal identity apart from my husband. In the English Department at the University of Louisville, I am Nancy Drown Allen, not Mike's wife. Recently a friend mentioned that he had heard about the Allens before meeting us. "What did you hear about us?" I asked. My friend said he'd heard that Mike was "bright." And I? "Well," he grinned, "you were just mentioned as 'his-lovely-wife-Nancy.' " God has helped me work through my wounded pride in these instances, because I know he has given me separate gifts of my own. Fortunately, he has also given me a husband who applauds my every success, soothes my failures, and dulls the stings of insensitive peers. In doing this, Mike has discovered a secret. Just as I can feel pride in sharing his success, he has found pride in my success.

An outgrowth of Mike's pride in me is his participation in my career. For years women have done what was expected of them in social situations—having the boss for dinner, playing bridge with the wives of his associates, or being the perfect minister's wife. Now Mike finds that he is expected to attend English Department parties and horse shows. This he has done willingly, and several months ago our entire family spent much of a weekend inside a large shopping mall in Louisville where horses were being displayed. Mike helped with the promotion; our two sons played with the ponies; and I interviewed people. We had more time together—and more fun—that weekend than most!

I have learned that there is some grace in merely enduring. God is still the God of job searches, tears in the bathroom, and dirt on the kitchen floor. I have a renewed faith in myself with the feeling that God has a place for me in the world. I can teach people. I can help people. And while I am doing this, I am setting an example for my two sons. Their world will not be as limited as the one Mike and I grew up in. The *norm* for them is a mother who works inside and outside the home, a father who works inside and outside the home, and happy (sometimes) parents who love them (all the time)! Not only am I *still* a homemaker, but Mike is, too. But we are also breadwinners.

With Mike's graduation approaching in another year, we must face the reality of another moving crisis. I occasionally remember the day that—after the long job search—I taught my first class at Indiana University Southeast. Walking out into the bright sunshine, I looked up and thanked God for that class, with tears welling up in my eyes. I knew I was in the right place. Mike and I may never have an easy solution for deciding who moves when the job opportunity comes, but I hope we'll always be able to feel that we've come to the right place.

****

Nancy Allen teaches English composition at two universities and edits a horse magazine in her spare time. She and her husband, Mike, who live in Louisville, Kentucky, patiently parent Matthew and Eric, ages eight and ten. She and Mike teach singles in Sunday School. Nancy also likes to ride horses, read books, and work in political campaigns.

10

Career Interruption

Margaret Mein Graves

Many times in the past three years, at a party or a meeting, during the time of introductions, I have found myself wondering what to say that I do. I noticed that other women have some of the same discomfort. Many times my husband has introduced me as the past director of a well-known senior citizens' program. All of this ambiguity about what I do lies in the fact that for these past few years I have not been gainfully employed but have chosen to stay home and take the daily responsibility of caring for our son.

A few years ago I would have been expected to assume the role of full-time mother when our children were born. I might even have been considered a "bad" mother if I didn't give up my own personal professional ambitions to become a full-time caregiver. Fortunately, the expectations have changed. Now it is acceptable for us as women to pursue our educational and career goals while being wife and mother. As in many other areas, the added opportunities I am given as a woman mean more choices I need to make and for which I must assume the responsibility. For me, the choices were between being a professional with a family or choosing to interrupt my career and stay home full-time with our child.

Our past as well as present situations play important roles in the decisions we make. My parents assumed rather traditional male and female family roles, although they did not always seem to fit society's mold. My mother was the one in the family from whom neighbors would borrow tools; she could fix anything. My father was the person who attracted young children and seemed most affectionate to his own. There were three children in our family, and our parents encouraged each of us to pursue our own interests. They considered our completion of academic degrees very important. As a teenager I remember many times being asked to promise to finish college before getting married. As I neared the end of college and made application for entrance into seminary, my father was very supportive of that choice. He encouraged me, when others around were saying it wasn't really done, to enter the divinity degree program. There also were several people outside my family who gave me stong encouragement during my college and seminary years. They made me feel that I could achieve in my own areas of interest and had something unique to offer as a woman pursuing a career in a male-dominated field.

After finishing a master's degree at the seminary I became director of an adult day center. In that position I became aware of the skills I have in administration, recruitment, and personnel management.

However, at the end of three years of work at the center, I decided to retire from my professional life for a time and become full-time mother to the child that we were having.

This decision, although appearing relatively easy to make, had to be carefully thought out. After all the money and emotional investment made by my parents, other support persons, and myself in my education and career goals, it seemed a waste to put a halt to all of that to stay home full-time with a child. I felt at times that I was possibly cheating those people who had encouraged me so strongly in my earlier years.

Also, my husband, unlike many men, feels very favorably about women working outside the home. To him it was not imperative that I make the decision to quit and stay at home full-time. Apart from feelings, the practical aspects of our family finances had, of course, to enter into my decision. If we are very careful financially we are able to be a one-salary family.

Our son is now almost three, and we are awaiting the birth of our second child. I feel that my decision to do full-time mothering was right for us when I initially made it, and I continue to feel that it is the course I need to follow for at least a few more years. The occasional economic strain is difficult and makes me reevaluate my choice more than any other aspect of our lives.

My decision in favor of career interruption is based primarily on the belief I have that very young children need the nurturing and bonding which can best be given when there is at least one person consistently loving and attached to that child. Since so much of what children become as adults intellectually and emotionally depends on their experiences in their first few years of life, I decided that I would try to be as good a parent as I possibly could be, and for me that meant doing it full-time during the children's early years.

Since I grew up in a Christian home, the support of our church community became very important to me during this time. About the time that our son was born, my husband and I moved our membership back to Crescent Hill Baptist Church. In this fellowship we have found real support for what we do as individuals and a real affirmation of the gifts we can uniquely offer. It is within our church structure that I have been able to continue to use some of the skills I had developed professionally. Serving on various church committees, I have assisted with the organization of women's retreats, have taught in several children's programs, and have spearheaded the start of an after-school daycare program for elementary children in our community. As a part of a Christian church family I have often felt that not only were our needs as parents being met; but I have also felt the love and support of the community for our son through the programs offered him and from individuals who give him nurture and attention.

Many women seem to experience a feeling of isolation from other adults as they leave the job market and find themselves at home full-time with a child. To be an effective full-time parent I realize the need for my own self to be nourished and stretched. One of the ways I consistently found this opportunity right after our son James was born was through a group of other mothers of infants who had taken the initiative to meet with each other weekly for a time of mutual support and fellowship. This group, which occasionally changed in personality makeup and format, met together in each others' homes for about two years. There were weeks when we just enjoyed each others' company while our children played. There were other times when we were ministers to the needs of one of us by listening with the ears of a friend. At times we had formal discussions on topics related to childrearing or took short field trips for the fun of being out as a group. This formalized group as well as some less structured relationships have been meaningful for the emotional support necessary during this time.

Another way that I have found to feel less isolated from other adults and which also helps our financial situation has been to baby-sit for one or two children on a regular basis. These have been children of friends whose mothers either have chosen or have been forced to work outside the home. By keeping these children I provided a caring enviroment for them, built-in companionship for my son, and a constant contact between other adults and myself.

The time that I have had at home with our son has been invaluable. I feel that because I have been with him consistently during these first few years, he is developing into a person with good self-esteem who has a feeling of being truly loved and the ability to love the people around him. I hope that these characteristics will endure into his adult years.

Because my life has not been dictated by the time constraints of an outside job our time at home during the day has been very flexible. This meant that I could nurse him for many months. I could also stop a household task if there was a book he wanted to read or another project we needed to do together. Walks out of doors, whatever the season, have been a part of our day since he was a tiny baby. If there is a pretty day it has been so nice to plan impromptu trips to the zoo to see his favorite animals. Because the amount of time I have to get housekeeping jobs done is flexible, I can take the time to let James help with them. As a toddler he loves housekeeping much more than I do. He learned to vacuum and wash dishes for fun! He loves to "cook" (when he makes a mess I remind myself we won't have these times together forever).

Because James and I spend this time together each day, the evening and weekend times when my husband David is at home is a special time to share as a family or for James and his dad to be together.

We garden as a family, and our son takes special interest not only in the planting of seeds and upkeep of the garden but also in picking and eating what he had planted weeks before. He and David spend time together doing odd jobs around the house, working in the yard, reading together, or building with blocks.

During the time James spends with his father or during an occasional baby-sitting exchange, I have tried to take the time I need to pursue my own interests for my personal growth, whether these be reading, sewing, community activities, or personal retreats. Disciplining myself to develop and grow in these areas is a goal I constantly keep before me.

The choice which I made three years ago was to stay home full-time with our son. Although I am already looking at the available job market and my career educational requirments for the future, I feel that my decision still stands for the present. Each time I re-think my decision I realize I want to continue to live with the one I have made.

****

Margaret Graves gave birth to a second son, Tom, just after completing this chapter. Son James was already in the picture, as was husband David. Margaret works with international students (she was born on the mission field in South America), has organized a food cooperative, and enjoys working at church and in the community. The Graves family lives in Louisville, Kentucky.

11

Identity

Judy Grabiel Gaddy

The doctoral thesis had been completed and accepted. The Southern Baptist Theological Seminary had awarded the degree. A church had issued an invitation for Welton to come as pastor. *We* had accepted.

The time had come to tell the news to our friends at First Marion Baptist Church in Seymour, Indiana. They had fed us, nurtured us, cared for us, and, after six years, come to love us as we did them. We called Eugene Engle and his wife Mildred. They had provided ham salad sandwiches, potato chips, and Big Red nearly every Sunday night while Welton served as pastor to their rural church. Most of the congregation shared a party line, so we knew that one telephone call would inform the entire community. We told them that Beechwood Baptist Church had called Welton to serve as pastor. Questions and answers were exchanged: "What size is it?" "Where is it located?" "When will you move?" and finally Eugene asked, "Do they know Judy yet?"

Our friend's good-natured tease relieved the tension. However, it was a very significant question. The only more important question would have been, "Does Judy know herself yet?"

I knew well who I had been—the daughter of Russell and Julia Grabiel, the younger sister of Mary Elizabeth, the older sister of

Harriet Jo, Betty Sue, and Mitzi Lou. Within our "house of seven Grabiels" we girls received valuable gifts as children. Each of us was accepted as a unique individual, helped to find personal identity, and encouraged to be herself. Our home was one of healthy competition, conflict, and diverse interests, held together by mutual love. On every subject or idea there were at least five opinions. After all, we were the offspring of a staunch Democratic mother and a rabid Republican father. In retrospect, this Methodist home provided an excellent setting for the rearing of a Baptist pastor's wife. Here, biblical truths were taught and ethical living expected as well as encouraged.

I never intended to marry a minister. In fact, I did not. I married the boy with the curly black hair and dark brown eyes who worked across the aisle from me in chemistry lab. Even though I made better grades than he, he seemed always to know the right answers and why those answers were right. I suspected he had more intelligence than he was willing to use. Welton was a good friend whom I could ask for help with an assurance that he would respond in as positive a manner as possible. We did not date until the last of our senior year. We saw little of each other during our freshman year at a small state university near our hometown. Welton spent most of his time at the BSU Center; I was very involved as a cheerleader. No one was terribly surprised when Welton announced that he was transferring to Union University, a Baptist college, or that he intended to enter the ministry.

In March of 1960, Welton was ordained. On the day of the ordination service, he gave me a white Bible with a lengthy letter written on the first page. Among other things, he wrote, "With this goes all the love I have to give." I believed every word of it. In the last twenty-one years, I have never doubted that he meant it.

We were married after our junior year in college. I did not return to school that first year. There was plenty to do in our petite apartment. I cooked three meals a day, waxed the floors every week, made draperies to cover the doorless closets, and listened sympathetically to our friends as they discovered they were going to become parents soon after graduation. Every weekend we went to our church located just outside of Paris, Tennessee.

Welton and I decided that I had to keep the promise made to my parents and return to college. We were also committed to his getting a seminary education. Neither of us knew how we would keep these commitments, but they were made. After checking into colleges in Louisville, where the seminary was located, we knew it would be too expensive for me to finish school out of my home state. The church in Paris really wanted Welton to continue as pastor. I could get a scholarship at University of Tennessee at Martin. My sister, who was teaching there, offered to share her home with me. A way emerged.

Our decisions meant that Welton would have to travel from Louisville, Kentucky, to Paris, Tennessee, every Friday night and return on Monday morning. This was made simpler when the L and N Railroad gave Welton a weekend pass. He had eight hours of uninterrupted study time and even typed papers on the trips. We worked hard five days a week and honeymooned every weekend for those nine months. Our grades were never better. Though I would not recommend this life-style for everyone, it worked for us. We both realized that my ego would never tolerate the blow of not finishing college. I needed the degree in order to accomplish other goals. This was the first time we tested the equality of our marriage; the arrangement was not *easy* for us, but it was *right* for us.

The next seven years were much more traditional. My teaching position was at Parkland Junior High School in Louisville, an inner-city school in a poverty area. These years were difficult for our country nationally. Everyone felt strongly about everything. During the sixties, classrooms were not isolated from the riots, confusion, hate, and unrest that disrupted our cities. I was emotionally exhausted from trying to keep order, much less teach children who were hungry, disturbed, abused, and really without a reason to trust anyone.

Seminary days were as influential as they were memorable. In this community of faith, I formed substantive ideas about the church and grappled with the myths and mandates of life as a pastor's wife. The friendships of those years have proved to be our most enduring ones. Our two sons were born in Louisville. While there Welton was recommended to our church in Paris Crossing, Indiana.

That church was to be our primary Christian fellowship for six years. Members of the congregation tolerated our mistakes, accepted our contributions, and allowed us to grow with them as we worked together learning about God's will. For me, more often than not, the divine directive seemed to be "wait a while." I supposed the waiting would end upon Welton's completion of the doctoral program.

Finally that idea was tested. We accepted a call to Beechwood Baptist Church in Louisville, Kentucky. We moved from our Seminary Village apartment to Wildwood Lane. Our first house! At long last Welton could be the *perfect pastor* and I the *perfect wife*. A diligently held dream was about to be realized.

Beechwood was even better than we had expected. The congregation was filled with good people eager to cooperate and willing to work. Beechwood was our Camelot. My dreams and Welton's special gifts were so complementarily meshed with the needs of these people that had it been God's will, we would still be there. Like all Camelots, however, it was short-lived. After two years, Welton accepted a position with the Christian Life Commission of the Southern Baptist Convention.

While we lived in Nashville we experienced the flip side of the pastorate. Choosing a church home was the single most difficult decision that we had to make in those four years.

For the first time we had to make friends apart from leadership roles. Absent were those instantly receptive people to welcome a pastor and his family. We had to pick Sunday School classes and take a backseat. No one even suspected that we had just left the perfect church with all the answers. Finally, though, we could sit together and learn how to worship together as a family.

During this period I learned something very important about my relationship to the church. I was somewhat surprised to discover that all these years we had not been going to church because it was expected of us but because we truly wanted to and needed to. A special joy came when Welton was ordained as a deacon and I accepted the presidency of the WMU and worked with the children's Mission Friends.

After four years of working at the Christian Life Commision, Welton was called to pastor Broadway Baptist Church in Fort Worth, Texas. I knew God had not remembered the promise I had made a long time ago. I promised to try my hardest to be the best pastor's wife possible if he would not send us to the foreign mission field—and that included Texas!

The pulpit committee from Broadway was the most sensitive, best-informed, and diverse group of Christian people a church could assemble. I realize now that the success of this committee was that they truly represented the body of Christian people they were sent out to serve. I could hardly wait to get to Texas.

Through the years I encountered hand-me-down myths of a pastor's wife. Some of these are so ridiculous as to qualify as jokes. However, many are hurtful because they have been commended as ideals by "how-to" books written for a "successful" pastor's wife. Just as my past history tells me who I am, the myths help me know who I am not.

The first myth to go was that of some stylized person known as *the* pastor's wife. A woman may be married to a man who is a minister; however, no woman's identity can come from her husband's occupation. Any woman who tries to follow someone else's idea of her role is bound to lead an uncomfortable existence. To perform acceptably she must look outside her own needs, abilities, and talents as well as her family's.

People who accept such a dictated life-style have great difficulty. They not only have trouble remembering who they were but almost never know who they have become until they are so filled with inner conflicts that they can no longer live within themselves. Those they love become burdens. Life is uncomfortable for all. This is why I am more convinced than ever that personal identity is more important than professional role. It is imperative to know who you are.

Myth number two is the most disturbing—"You cannot have close friends." Perhaps if friendship is confused as fellowship with a gossip partner, the counsel is wise. However, our closest friends have always been members of the congregation. Some of our best friends ever were not only church members but a deacon's family who lived next door. With these neighbors, we shared meals, interests, hobbies, and recreation (everything from a half a cup of flour to a full cup of comfort). Early in our pilgrimage, we learned to trust our *own* ideas and feelings about with whom we would spend our time. We have never let anyone choose our friends for us.

Professionally, we always accept the first invitation extended to us. We do not have to justify how or with whom we spend our time. This makes great demands upon our time; however, both my husband and I enjoy being with a lot of people . . . all kinds of people . . . all ages of people.

Another myth rejected is that "You can't (or should not if you could) get too close to staff members." We regularly have get-togethers for staff members and their spouses or dates. These occasions form some of our most enjoyable times. We have been fortunate to be able to associate with staff friends who share our feelings about the importance of times together.

Perhaps the cruelest and most destructive myth passed on to pastor's wives is the one about preacher's children being the meanest children in the congregation. I cringe every time I hear this one.

Probably the opposite idea of having to be better because of dad's being a preacher is more hurtful to our sons. Our boys are neither meaner nor better because of who their father is or because of his position. They are themselves. Each one is unique. Each one brings his own special gifts and problems into our home and into our church. We do not dictate participation in every church-related event.

Our older son decided he had rather work in the sound room than sing in the choir. He convinced us that he sincerely felt this was just as viable a service. We accepted his decision.

Decisions constantly have to be made about Wednesday night athletic events and Sunday afternoon football games. Each situation is treated individually with attention being given to the importance of the event, previous commitments, and responsibilities, as well as wishes.

Our fourteen-year-old was obviously surprised a couple of years ago when we gave him permission to go to a dance. His friends at school had convinced him that Baptists do not believe in dancing.

A related myth—which if true would give justification for believing the former one—is that preacher's families suffer because no time is available for togetherness. Quite honestly, this myth is often dangerously close to reality. My husband has the inclination to fill every waking moment with some activity—usually work. Both of us recognized this very early in his ministry. Consequently, we tried to be sure that a full schedule included activities all of us could enjoy.

Our times away have been filled with long drives along scenic routes, long walks, and time for just us. Outings like these have helped us through some very difficult periods. Invariably we feel stronger and better prepared for coping when we return.

Time for husband and wife togetherness needs the complement of times for parent-children togetherness. While our older son was still a baby, we adjusted his sleeping schedule so he would be awake at those times when his dad was home. Of course, we also had those long weekend drives together on our way to the church in Indiana. Then in Louisville, while Welton pastored at Beechwood, John Paul attended the church's nursery school. The two of them journeyed to the church together every morning, sometimes even sharing an early morning breakfast on their way. Time for one-to-one experiences with each of the boys is difficult but essential. Since all of our family likes sports, we find lots of places to go and things to do together.

Both boys have the number of their dad's private telephone at the office. Because they know they can reach him any time they want to or need to, they do not abuse the privilege. On several occasions I have overheard one side of a conversation such as, "Dad, Hollywood Henderson has just been cut." At those times I admit to feeling some guilt about infringements on valuable time. However, more dominant is a feeling of gratitude for a father-son relationship in which the boys assume that their dad is most interested in the most important things on their minds. He usually is.

A myth about which we have often laughed states that the preacher's wife must be able to play the piano. For years I felt like a child with only one talent in a world full of multi-talented kids. I was not even sure what that one talent was. I still feel a cold shudder when someone asks, "And what do you do?" I immediately reassess my can'ts and don'ts—I don't sing; I am not a gifted scholar; I don't play the piano; I'm not a beautiful redhead; and so on.

Even more difficult to explain are my competencies. I am an excellent wife and a fairly good mother; I sew better than most; and I can sniff out the cheapest ground beef in the city. Of course, I know all of that does not add up to make a ten-talent person. I hate to admit it, but these confessions come close to positioning me as one of those pastor's wives whose life sounds domesticated and dull. I am domesticated but I am not *dull*. As a matter of fact, I have finally discovered my gift.

The personal pilgrimage which I have enjoyed and the "professional myths" which I have encountered and explored have helped me discover the gift with which I am endowed and the meaning by which my life is characterized. You have noticed an excessive use of "we," though this article is about me. That is intentional. A major part of my life involves my husband and his ministry. Yet, who I am is not dictated by who he is or what he does. I am a person first. I am a pastor's wife as well. Meaning for me comes not from role but from identity.

One day when Mary Cosby and I were having lunch, she asked me the previously dreaded question, "What do you feel are your gifts?" I attempted to describe for her my contributions to family, church, God, and country. Suddenly, a terrific expression of excitement showed on her face. Mary announced, "Oh, you are a facilitator!" What good news! Deep in my heart I knew that not everyone has this unique gift. It is special and I have it. I also acknowledged to myself what I have always known. Most important among women's needs are not identities dictated by their husband's professions—"pastors' wives" included—but persons whose identities are governed by their gifts. Maybe what this world needs are more facilitators. And I am one!

****

Judy Gaddy has been and is a mother, pastor's wife, and creative individual. She is very active in Broadway Baptist Church, Fort Worth, Texas, where husband Welton pastors. Judy plays tennis, swims, and coordinates schedules for John Paul and James Welton.

12

Mid-Life
Anita Bass

When does mid-life start? Is it when the
  —steps seem steeper?
  —print seems smaller?
  —speakers mumble?
  —policemen look younger?
  —nest is empty?
  —body parts sag?
  —lines appear on the face?
  —young people seem so taut, virile, and inviting?
  —friends and family begin to die?
  The age at which one or more of the above begins varies from person to person. It may depend on the genes. It may depend on the climate, the culture, or cold cream.
  For me the realization of the approaching of middle age was when my husband Roy and I had been to the fifteenth reunion of his college class. You know how those things go—people try to look their most prosperous and successful best. It works better for some than it does for others. It was Roy's succinct observation that the difference between the classy and good-looking ones and the "also rans" was "The Three P's: Posture, Pounds, and Primping."
  With a perceptive husband like that I bought into that "Three

P Theory," and I all but wore them on my forehead. That idea gave me a goal which in turn gave me a sense of worth and self-esteem. It required discipline for the Pounds because I tend to be chunky, plump, round—aw, I really mean fat! I conducted charm classes for young women and girls in our church and local women's groups. That kept me alert to Posture and Primping. Oh, yes—it was along about then that I began having a lot of gray hair, but "only my hairdresser knew."

Since I was twenty-eight, thirty, and thirty-two years old when I had our three sons, I did not consider a mid-life crisis at forty. I was too busy working on my Three Ps and being a working mother. I worked at running an efficient and effective household; I worked at being a loyal and supportive wife; I worked at being a neighborly neighbor; I worked at being mother to our three sons and a niece who lived with us part-time.

I also worked at the church as Sunday School superintendent, president of a Baptist Women's group, and choir member; and I hosted a Bible study that met in our home every Thursday for fifteen years. I was responsible for the lesson only the first four years; after that a person on the church staff took responsibility for teaching.

I worked as a volunteer in the community at the retirement home, museum, hospital child welfare agency, and crippled children's program.

I did work for money when I directed weddings, sang in funeral home quartets, led seminars on Love-Courtship-Marriage, taught charm classes, and wrote articles for periodicals. I also worked for an interior designer during the hours the children were in school. It was rewarding to me to put my salary into a trust fund for our sons. We labeled it "Funds for Adventure and Permanent Improvements." That fund afforded all three of them trips abroad. They also bought diamonds and wedding rings and a few other "permanent improvements."

My physical health was excellent. My energy level was high.

And, reflecting on the previous paragraphs—*I must have been healthy!* I never complained. I loved my life and had little understanding for those who seemed not to be as fizzy. I even had the gall to suspect that young women who complained at childbirth and older women who talked of menopausal symptoms were trying to get the attention of their husbands, kids, or doctors. I changed my tune when I had a "hot flash" at fifty. I knew I was having a stroke or some fatal attack and called my doctor immediately. He told me I was normal and merely experiencing mid-life symptoms and assured me it was seldom fatal! A big lesson for me to learn—change of life is a reality!

I'm glad that I did not know how difficult my fifth decade would be or I would have been miserably debilitated. I would have had agoraphobia as described by Dr. Paul Tournier. He says that to be caught in the middle, not having a feeling of security to the beginning or to the end, is to have agoraphobia. In retrospect, it was God's grace that I did not know what mid-life held for me.

It all seemed to begin when our last child left for college. We had very few rigid rules at our house, but one rule was that going to college meant going out of town. We felt our sons needed to learn how to manage their own time, money, car, laundry, and studies. The youngest left! Empty nest! We even had a celebration dinner with dedicatory prayers by each of us to mark our new era.

As if by magic the curtain went up the next week, and the first scene was a placard which read: "Middle age is that time when one is caught between the dependent children and the aging parents." Our parents began to have broken bones, strokes, surgeries, and emotional problems which required our time and concern. On the other hand, we had our sons who required our financial and emotional support.

I suddenly realized I was not equipped for my fifties. I had read a lot about children and about the elderly, but I had not heard much about mid-life, and that was my place now. Roy, too, seemed unsettled and began to talk about a new direction and changes he would like to make.

We saw a psychologist who tested and evaluated us. We worked on some of our problems with him and heard his suggestions for us. Of the many things he told us, two things were most surprising: First, Roy had aptitudes and abilities in the area of politics; second, I had a high need for personal accomplishment and recognition. We chuckled, knowing that politics would never be a part of our lives and that I had already received personal recognition in church and community.

We were to find later that was not exactly true.

As we were staggering around trying to find direction and being dutifully helpful to our parents and children, we had occasional trips and rewards. Then that time came that comes in all families when they take on new persons and new dimensions. For us it was three weddings in five years. The first two sons married during their first years of law school, and the third son married in his second year after undergraduate work; a good deal of trauma was associated with the three new members of our family.

I hasten to say we liked the wives. They were bright, beautiful women. I regret that I did not deal skillfully with many of the crises involving them. They taught me a lot. I am still learning from them. It helps me now to know they have forgiven me for my stupidities. I am glad God has also forgiven me for my sins of those days. I like to think God makes a mosaic out of our brokenness, and I gave him lots of pieces during those years!

Then came the decision whether or not I should be ordained as a deacon in our church. I accepted the responsibility but was uncomfortable since only one other church in our state had ordained women deacons.

I had my share of negative remarks. I consider classic the one made to me by a man from another state: "I hope to God I die before they ordain women in my church." I thanked him for feeling comfortable enough with me to speak his mind. I then changed the subject, which is often my avoidance tactic when things get tense.

One of my characterological flaws!

When I was ordained as a deacon I certainly had not anticipated that I would be the chairperson of the group within two years. I had a three-year term in that capacity. I had to relate to many committees and tried to implement many new programs. Therefore, it was one of the hardest jobs I had. The willing support and enthusiasm from church members enabled me to carry out my task.

Another new and invigorating experience came for me when I was elected to a four-year term as one of the five persons from my state to the Southern Baptist Convention Executive Committee. The committee is composed of sixty-four persons who meet in regular session three times a year. I was one of five women on the committee. I quickly got a feeling of what it's like to be part of a minority. I felt excluded and ignored for the first two meetings. Only a few "secure-type" men would be seen talking to me. I accepted the challenge by being low-key and by doing my homework on the agenda items. I made motions and spoke out when I felt it appropriate.

That job improved my prayer life! Roy was supportive and encouraging. I am glad to say that by the second year the men were gracious and accepting. The third year I chaired a subcommittee. The fourth year I chaired the Business and Finance Committee. This is one of three major divisions of the Executive Committee. I became the first woman ever to chair one of these divisions. It was rewarding to me to have rapport and response from every committee member. I regret I was unable to accept the invitation for another four-year term, since I like being a productive, contributing person.

In the middle of our mid-life Roy fulfilled the prophecy that he would be a good politician. He ran for mayor of our town of 175,000 at the behest of our number one son and got elected by 64 percent of the votes. He was reelected for another two-year term by an 81 percent majority. He was altruistic to the core in wanting to repay a town that had been good to him. He was a popular, fair, and effective mayor. He included me in everything possible, and I enjoyed representing our community at numerous events at home and other places such as Atlanta, San Francisco, Washington, New York, and London. We also made personal trips to Europe, Norway, Sea Isle, and Santa Fe. Mid-life was not so bad! In fact, we felt ourselves approaching the next era secure.

Roy died suddenly one mid-December Saturday afternoon.

Shattered dreams!

Shattered life!

My first response was, "Honey, what have you done to me?" For Roy had been my strength. He had cajoled, encouraged, and pushed me to take jobs, make speeches, write articles. He assured me of my abilities and would always say, "You can do it, and I'll help you." And he would. How could he help me now in this terrifying and trying time?

The enveloping love of God became real to me in a few hours, and Roy's presence and strength seemed real. I felt it, though I cannot explain it. I was able to go through the funeral and burial, and ten days later I had major surgery. I then stayed in my house for a month and dealt with my grief and recuperated from the surgery. I saw selected people. The deacons, our Sunday School group, and the Thursday Bible study group were God's beautiful comforters to me.

I began a brand-new career a few months after Roy's death. I am hostess for a thirty-minute TV show five days a week. When I began I was unsure of myself, since all of my training and experience had been with live audiences and platform performances. The nonresponding camera scared me. I often needed Roy to nudge me along—and he did! I now have that personal recognition in a surprisingly different but affirming way.

Tragedies have continued to stalk my path: My father died. A dear friend died. Several close friends moved away. I underwent another surgery recently. One of the three marriages in our family ended in divorce, and I have desperately missed my six-year-old granddaughter. She moved with her mother several hundred miles away.

Some beautiful things have also happened. Before Roy died he had a grandson named for him. That child has been a beautiful reminder to me of Roy's strong-willed gentleness. We had two other baby boys born last summer. I was privileged to be in the delivery rooms for the sacred happenings. Life goes, but life comes.

I am now a widow.

I have hated that word! I no longer wear my wedding band. I took it off after eighteen months. For me it was a symbol of living in the past. Taking that ring off meant that both Roy and I are now fully free to be on about our growth, he in his place with God and me here in the world.

What about the Three Ps? I am still using that theory to try to make the most of what God gave me. I weigh the same. I exercise, "suck-in" and stand tall. I regularly update my makeup and hairstyle. I may even have a face-lift. Who knows? I am in a growth group that has helped me with periodic times of depression and with some significant decisions.

I occasionally have an evening with a man friend. I enjoy my friends and families, my church, career, and community.

Was that mid-life?

Mid-life was what?

It was a scary, grievous, painful, but enriching and enlightening journey. At times I did not think I would survive it, but I am glad I did not miss it because I think it made a real person out of me. I recommend it for everybody. Maybe it won't be as rugged for you!

I am now not at the beginning or the middle. I am toward the end. I look forward to the creative days I have until the end of this existence and the new existence in God's presence when growth will continue. Doxology! See you there!

Shalom!

****

Anita Bass can be seen on television as a talk show host in her hometown of Lubbock, Texas. She serves as a trustee for various Baptist educational institutions, as a deacon in her local church, and as a volunteer in community agencies.

13

Singleness

Mary H. Risinger

I didn't start out to build a single life. As a matter of fact, I didn't start out to *build* a life at all. What I had in mind was living out my own personal version of a textbook marriage and family relationship, complete with tall, handsome husband, two charming children, several pets, and a house that kept itself clean. My unconscious expectation was that all of this would miraculously start falling into place around age twenty-five, about the time I finished my studies at The Southern Baptist Theological Seminary. It would be a sort of cosmic graduation present, my reward for studying hard, making friends with only the nicest people, and generally being such a good girl.

The problem was that age twenty-five found me staggering out of a wrenching relationship that was supposed to have been God's will, getting graduated out of a community that had become home to me, and searching for some sort of socially acceptable job to occupy my time until God realized his tardiness in delivering my life's plan. I was frightened, confused, anxious, depressed, and essentially paralyzed as I began to face the question, "What do I do now?" I never knew that bewilderment could hurt so badly. What on earth could have gone so wrong? I, the child spared from death at thirteen months, the gifted one, the "holy" one, the rock of my family and the nurturer of my friends, found that I simply had no skills with which to orchestrate a single life. I had no knowledge that I had a life, other than the one which I had constructed out of other people's and my own fantasy expectations.

Without my fantasy self (the good-girl-turned-perfect-wife-and-mother), I found that I had no self at all. That realization was terrifying. From my view, there was no "me" inside me. I have vivid memories of looking into a mirror and seeing nothing; of being spoken to by a co-worker and wondering why he talked to an empty hallway; of literally having no voice to utter my pain. Clearly, survival meant discovering something, a "someone" inside me who was no fantasy person. There had to be a "me" which didn't depend on a status related to somebody else, and I had to find her.

So instead of a newlywed saga after graduation, I began writing a chapter of my life known as "Beginning to Discover Mary." I did not "discover Mary," as if she were some sort of full-blown "together" person who simply had been hiding. Nor was I able to play at the search as if discovering my missing self was an entertaining pastime. I *began* to discover Mary—a process made infinitely more frightening by the fact that I had no idea what the outcome might be. Through individual and group counseling, through the support of family and loving friends, through hard work and commitment, I began a process of both discovering and developing a self—a Mary whom I could know and like and love and who could relate in a meaningful way to the people and events of her world, regardless of her marital status. Unprepared as I was, the process started out being almost scarier than I could face; but on this side of yesterday's vacuum, I've found the discovering to be continuous, challenging, exciting, and really kind of fun.

One of the biggest barriers to developing my self or discovering the fullness of myself was my rigid and/or limited understanding of God. I only knew a God of rules, expectations, and "oughtness." Following *that* image, I kept myself bound by expectations of a marriage that "ought" to happen. Or perhaps I had the roles switched and had created a God in my own restricted image. Perhaps both. The fact is that I had a lot of ideas and knew a lot of words about God, but I had no experiences from which I could identify his love for my real self—whoever she was. I had the form of a self, but possessed none of my own content with which to make a real life.

My two years as a seminary student helped me begin to do something about the hollowness I was feeling. Stripped of all my old assumptions about God, I grasped at ideas and insights I remembered from classes of the previous two years. Drawing from my theological studies, I began to shape a new understanding of God. Lessons from a half-dozen other classes helped me apply those theological understandings to human nature in general and to myself in particular.

Coming to a clearer and broader understanding of the nature of God was the cornerstone from which I was able to begin building the rest of my life. Pivotal concepts such as grace, mercy, and unconditional love had been religious vocabulary to me. They now became names for who God is. I remembered hours spent in counseling classes where we discussed models of good parenting and the significance of parental figures in a person's development. Slowly, then, my God of rules and expectations became the Dad of the prodigal and a poor shepherd stumbling through the darkness after one dumb sheep. All of the Sunday School lessons and Training Union parts and prayers I had ever heard began to make sense to me. For the first time I heard and knew in my soul that "Our Father" does not mean "Dear Sir."

Once I had established the identity and nature of God the Father, I began to explore the attributes of my self, many of which had been hidden by the old fantasy person. Taking my seminary lessons about human personality seriously, I began to experience and own *all* of my emotions. For the first time in my life, I felt free—free to be hurt and angry and scared as well as to be strong and nice and good. My newly emerging self got in touch with a power that I never had before—the power of my real self. It felt good.

With my "child of the Father" identity established and my newly discovered freedom of self, I burst forth as a theological adolescent of the first order. It became important for me to test the limits of my own emotional range and of my new relationship with unconditional love. I needed to know if I could be the whole of who I am and still be a "child of the Father." Could I trust him to love all of me? Could I be real and be loved for that?

Like the adolescent that I was, I began my God adventure tenuously at first. Soon, though, I tore about with true teenage recklessness. I allowed myself a full range of emotion, and I reveled or agonized in it all—the heights of devotion, piety, and commitment; the depths of despair and loneliness; the outer reaches of rage and defiance. I "let God have it" in occasional gratitude for a few things, but mostly in hostility and frustration for his failure to fulfill my "need" for a husband, home, and all-American lifestyle. I discarded my religious vocabulary and prayerful language and began having conversations with God which sounded like:

"I really don't like you much right now; but if you are who you say you are, then I guess you can handle that. If you can't I guess you're not God anyway."

"If you're such a loving God, how can you do _____ to me; or not do _____? How can you let _____ happen?"

"I'm so angry with you right now, and I feel so bad, that I'm not even going to talk to you. When I start feeling better, then maybe I'll talk to you again."

In short, I raged and cried and swore and threw tantrums and sulked and blamed God for all of my shattered dreams, disappointments, and pain. In my secret heart, however, I was hoping against hope, and in fact trusting, that God the Model Parent could and would endure my adolescence and be waiting for his child to grow up. Months later I finally began to lose my need to test God and my new self. I emerged from my theological adolescence with the profound knowledge that my whole self was who God had known and loved all along; and thus, perhaps it was possible for me to live and function and have meaning by myself. And I knew that I didn't have to worry about not being married any more.

The fact still remained, however, that I hadn't planned to be single, which meant that it was a status I had to get used to. When I was honest with myself, I had to admit that most of my views of single persons, single women, family life, and childrearing were downright debilitating. Again, using my seminary classes and counseling sessions for guidance, I "got in touch with my power" as a decision maker and shaper of my own attitudes and behaviors. I did myself a favor by reexamining many of my life views, looking for new models and trying to make room for new and different relationships, roles, and experiences.

It was fairly easy to tackle the marriage myths I had been living with simply by listening to *everything* I heard from my married friends—not just the good things or things that supported what I already believed. What I heard was both positive and negative reports about marriage from people who were experiencing a whole range of feelings about marriage. I also heard my married friends describe their impressions of being single and living a single lifestyle. They assumed that the freedom of singleness brought the same mythical happiness, success, sexual freedom, and fulfillment which I had always attributed to marriage! Mainly what I heard was people making adjustments to the same truth that was beginning to dawn on me: The meaning and content of my life is going to be shaped much more drastically by the *kind* of person I am than it is by whether or not I have a marriage license.

Understanding that, it became fairly simple for me to focus my interest and energy on being a person whom I like and respect. "Marital status" is just one of many descriptive characteristics about me. I see myself as a person. That I am a single person is sometimes relevant to certain situations, but sometimes so is being a white person, or a smart person, or a tall person.

The biggest issues I had to deal with in accepting myself and in building a single life were those having to do with my sexual identity, having children, and living in a traditional family setting. Sexuality was an issue because of the two kinds of cultural images single women tend to have. I am neither a swinging single nor a prim, starchy "old maid." Finding a place to enjoy being a woman somewhere between those two options meant blazing a trail through uncharted territory. I've had lots of good help in doing that, though, from friends who have consistently loved me through all of my building phases, with no regard for my marital status. I've been enriched by both male and female friends who have refused to discount or to capitalize on my sexuality just because I'm "available." And I'm grateful to be living at this time of the women's movement. Raised consciousnesses among my friends and colleagues have expanded the horizons of my relationships with both sexes. My life is made immeasurably better by the fact that the women's movement has given cultural validity to the theological truth which was so hard for me to learn: My worth as a person is not derived from my being attached to a man.

Feeling good about being a woman and about my relationships with men sometimes has made it more difficult for me to deal with the prospect of not having a husband or children. I've found that among many of my single, female friends the whole issue of family is sensitive. I know at least one single woman who avoids close friendships with married people and simply refuses to talk about children and family because all of that is too painful a reminder that she is alone. While I have certainly shared her sense of loss, I have decided that cutting myself off from the majority of people in the world just because they are married will not, in the long run, make me feel better. I've never regretted that choice.

It has taken time, however, to make peace with my sexual needs, my childbearing/nurturing needs, and my intimacy needs. I agonized for a long time, thinking that I simply could not live without experiencing the intimacy of pregnancy and childbearing with a man whom I loved totally. As it became apparent that I might not ever experience that, I wasn't sure that I could live with the grief. It would be easy if I could say that I just grew out of wanting to have a child or that my grief has disappeared with time. I haven't and it hasn't.

I feel about my childlessness now in the same way that I've come to feel about never having been a majorette. From preschool days through college, I fantasized myself as the gorgeous, exciting star, forever at the head of a huge marching band. Being a majorette was my life dream for at least ten years. It was clearly the most wonderful thing that anybody could ever do. But for all the reasons that kids' dreams sometimes get lost in families, I never had baton twirling lessons, and I marched with my clarinet in the middle of the band, among a thousand other clarinets. I've never stopped wanting to be a majorette, and sometimes I still long to be back in those days of Might Have Been.

That's how it is with me and babies. Sometimes I still wish "if only" and wonder what my life would have been or would be like if I'd been a majorette . . . or a mom. I don't grieve about either dream very often any more, but the wistfulness does appear occasionally. When it does, I accept the grief as reconfirmation of both my human vulnerability and my femininity. Each is an entirely allowable and worthy grief, but neither is worth sabotaging the rest of my life as if those were the only worthwhile occupations in life.

The good news is that there have also been some notable changes and additions to my life that I never could have foreseen amidst all of the adjustments of my twenties. With the help of friends who are open and willing to try new models of relationships, I've learned to drop much of my Traditional Family Chauvinism. (TFC is the view that happiness can only be derived in a home with a dad, a mom, two kids, and a mortgage.) I have a friend who has always believed, "All of my friends should know each other." Thus, he has shared not only his wealth of friends with me, but has included and treated me as family in the important occasions of his life. The concept of "chosen family" has become both an expanded option in my life-style and an incredibly meaningful alternative to a traditional family structure.

Then I became an aunt. My old Birth-Child Chauvinism (BCC says that the only real relationships with children are achieved through labor pains), reinforced by unhappy single friends and threatened married ones, said that birthing a baby is the only way to truly nurture and relate meaningfully to a child. Without that, I am somehow forever excluded from one of life's most enriching experiences. I reject that perspective outright. It's the old Genetic Kid Myth brought to us by the same folks who brought us the Marriage Myth.

Citing genetic children as the only model for meaningful adult/kid relationships reminds me of John Claypool's sermon on the prodigal son. Claypool describes the prodigal as having committed two sins: First, he made the erroneous assumption that he was everything and abused the heritage and resources that he had. Then amidst his failures and destruction in the far country, he made the equally false, opposite assumption that he was nothing. Claypool points out that the prodigal was neither; he was a real entity somewhere in the middle—not everything but certainly more than nothing.

So it is with the aunt business. In no way would I ever say that being an aunt is the same as being a parent. I know that it is not, and I try to remain sensitive to the differences so that I don't overstep the appropriateness of my role. But I take being an aunt very seriously. It is not a substitute for, or second-class version of, parenting. It is its own entity, providing mutual gifts of love, acceptance, encouragement, and affirmation for all of us. Aunting is not parenting; but it's not nothing.

Again I think of some single friends who, having no children, refuse to relate to children at all. To that attitude, I can only respond with the way my life turned upside down the morning of September 9, 1976. I got the long-awaited call that Sarah Ruth-anne Foreman had joined us on the planet. An hour later, on the way to work, in the middle of I-64 rush-hour traffic, without warn-ing, I began to sob with the same overwhelming joy, pride, and gratitude with which I am sobbing even as I write about it now. Sarah is here, and nothing will ever be the same. I may not be a parent, but what difference does that make to the agony I feel as Sarah develops traits like mine which I don't feel are productive, or to my pride in her brilliance and creativity which are just like me! I'll never be persuaded that Sarah's and my relationship is qualitatively inferior because she's "not really mine." She is mine, and I am hers, and what we have is special.

Then, just as I thought I was an old hand at the kid business, Scott Michael arrived to teach my family for the first time how it is with boys. With his maleness—both gentle and strong—with age-less three-year-old wisdom, and with infinite patience, Scott has expanded my capacity to love and my ability to appreciate and enjoy his wonderful uniqueness.

I won't deny that my relationships with my kids (or with kids that I borrow from time to time) are my substitutes for having children of my own. That doesn't make the relationships any less real or valuable. Wise parents have never claimed to meet all of their children's needs, and I think it's important for Sarah and Scott to know that the gaps can be filled by other adults who love them deeply. In that way, the needs of all of us get attended to. We enrich each other.

Last October, friends heard me describe how much Scott "needed" the green satin lizard suit (complete with pointy scales and four webbed feet) which I made him for Halloween. Every-body, including me, knew that the accurate statement was that I needed to express my love for Scott by making him that special suit. I did it for me and hoped he'd share my joy. I had no idea that in January, when Halloween had long since faded as a significant event, I would pick up my phone to hear the unmistakable, impossibly low-pitched voice of my male child saying, "Aunt Mary, I'm a green lizard." To this day, I'm the only person on my block who talks to lizards on the phone. Why would I ever consider diminishing the wonderful gift Scott is to me, simply because I did not birth him?

In fact, why would I diminish my life at all just because I'm not married? It's the only life I have, and I'm trying to do my best with it. The past years haven't been "dreams come true" or "happily ever after," but they've given me some good tools. As long as I've got good tools, I'll keep on building.

****

Mary Risinger is a program administrator in employment and training services to economically disadvantaged persons. A seminary graduate and a committed Christian, she serves as a deacon and chairs the Pastoral Care Committee in her church in Louisville, Kentucky.

Epilogue

The people who told their stories in this book have at least two things in common. First, we are women. Although the experiences we have described are not unique to women, we felt that other women would relate to the way we have dealt with our experiences. Society expects different things from women than from men. We expect different things from ourselves. We are all learning what God expects from us. We thought these stories would have value told from the women's perspectives.

A second thing we have in common is our Christian faith. And because we believe that we are continuously changing as a result of our life experiences, we believe that God is at work in us. Some of the themes and teachings of our Christian faith have become especially meaningful. We state them for you here.

God Is a God of Hope. We could not have gone through our darkest hours without hope. It is a gift without which the journey would be impossible. We hope for many things: a deeper faith, a better life, more meaning, or simply to make it through the day. We are a people of faith, and hope is the gift that keeps us going.

God Is a God of Redemption. We see God at work in our lives to bring something about. We aren't just surviving; we are being redeemed. Something different is made of us when we go through life's dark nights. We don't think God has sent the tragedies or painful experiences to us, but we know he works to bring healing and growth out of them. We are being redeemed.

God Is a God of Individuals and Community. Each of us is responsible for her own life. Yet each of us as a Christian is told to "bear one another's burdens" and "love thy neighbor as thyself." We aren't alone on our journeys; God provides community among our fellow travelers. The women in this book told of the strength they gained through their Christian community. Now you, the reader, have shared in that community. We have shared life together.

You have within yourself an unwritten chapter of this book. Perhaps it has helped you to know that others have experienced similar crises, have taken risks in order to grow, are recovering from devastating losses or disappointments, and have found immense joy in daily living.

One of the themes that has run throughout the book has been that our pilgrimage continues through our lives with a cycle of risk, pain, healing, and celebration. Our ability to cope varies; our faith falters at times; our resources seem limited. Yet God is ever with us.

We journey on.